To Everything Good

To Everything Good
W. Kevin Wells

Cover photograph by Joyce G, posted on Unsplash, cc0 license, unsplash.com.

"Tree of Life" posted on pixaby.com, pixabay license.

Photographs by Ben White, Dewang Gupta, John Mccann, Ivan Aleksic, Lance Grandahl, Johannes Plenio, Annie Spratt, and "lost design", posted on Unsplash, cc0 license, unsplash.com.

Photograph by Candace McDanielPosted, posted on StockSnap, cc0 license, stocksnap.io.

"The Good Shepherd" by Bernard Plockhorst, in the Public Domain, posted on publicdomainpictures.net by Cynthia Stevens, cc0 license.

Library of Congress Control Number: 2022902396

ISBN: 979-8-9857417-2-8 (Paperback edition)
ISBN: 979-8-9857417-3-5 (eBook edition)

Second Edition 2023

Self-Published
W. Kevin Wells

To Valerie:
thank you for
your love and insights.

To my parents:
thank you for teaching
me truths from childhood.

To teachers,
Church leaders,
authors, and friends:
thank you for sharing your
knowledge and understanding of truths.

Contents

Preface   vii

Our Ultimate Potential

A Beautiful Teaching   3
The Plan of Progression and Happiness   11

Biblical Teachings of Our Potential

Follow Jesus   27
Salvation   35
Heirs and Joint Heirs   41
The Father, The Son, and Us   49
Become One   57
Eternal Life   67
Ears to Hear and Eyes to See   73

Practical Application

Truth and Evidences   87
Living by Faith   99
Repent and Obey, Now is Our Time   111
The Church of Jesus Christ—Today   131
Testimony   151
Closing Thoughts   155

Additional Items

Appendix 1, A Second Witness of Christ   165
Appendix 2, Religious Affiliation   167
Scripture Index   169

PREFACE

This book teaches our ultimate potential, the potential to become everything good—not that we must be perfect, neither that our worth depends upon good acts—rather, each individual can, because of God's plan, become as perfect as they deeply desire.

This potential is real. It is not sentimental feel-good glaze. We are on the earth to learn and become. Ultimately, some individuals will, after their time on earth, become everything that is good. This book shares this beautiful truth.

A second purpose of this book is to show that this doctrine is neither obscure nor strange, being plainly taught in the Bible.

A third purpose is to invite the reader to seek Jesus Christ and follow him. Jesus Christ is the way to everything good. Because of him, becoming perfect is more than a lofty aspiration.

I do not represent a religion, organization, or group in writing this book. I am responsible for the content, including any errors.

Errors and The Writer

While writing one cold winter evening, I spotted an error hiding behind the wood stove, enjoying the warmth. Reaching for the poker, I arose, intent on driving that error from my writing. It saw me coming and immediately split in two scampering left and right. I stomped left with my foot and swung the poker to the right. This caused the error to split again. I doubled my efforts with vigorous swings and forcible stomps, chasing errors up and down sentences. It seemed the error's purpose for existence was to multiply.

When the struggle ended, I replaced the stovepipe where it belonged and extinguished the embers about the room using the same foot used for stomping errors. A thorough search revealed I had won. No trace of that error existed. However, around the edges of the room stood new errors. They stared at me, confident enough to not hide.

Hopefully, any errors in this book are few and insignificant.

I present my understanding of truths that first inspired me when I was young. I've studied and pondered these truths throughout my life. I do not claim ownership of the doctrines presented. But I feel the reader will gain valuable insights from my contribution.

I quote many scriptures from the Holy Bible, but we need to be careful. Some people use scriptures in attempts to build creditable foundations underneath false teachings. The mere quoting of biblical verse does not prove true one's personal construction of beliefs, regardless of the beauty or prominence of the edifice.

Truth stands independent. Spiritual truths do not need documents to prove validity. Confirmation that we can become everything good comes from God, not from slinging scriptures around like affidavits in attempts to smother anyone who disagrees.

Because truth resonates with truth, correct teachings will always harmonize with God's revealed word. As you read this book any truths herein will vibrate in a reassuring melody consistent with God's word.

We can use scriptures to learn about and understand our potential. We can trust God to provide proof according to his methods and not try to force it ourselves. He is wiser than us.

When I insert comments within a scripture quote, I use brackets. I underlined words that give the gist of why the scripture is quoted. If desired, you can skim the quotes by reading only the underline words. This keeps the reading stream flowing. When you want to peruse deeper, the entire quote is there.

I hope you enjoy this book. I hope it enriches your understanding of our potential to become everything good.

W. Kevin Wells

OUR

ULTIMATE

POTENTIAL

A Beautiful Teaching

Mortal life has a beautiful underlying purpose. Our choices, like curves in a road, determine direction. The inner person, the person we really are, self-creates by the direction of our choices. Other people's actions and choices affect us; we don't decide everything about our own life. But the underlying road we travel, who we are and who we are becoming, takes shape by what we choose.

Heavenly Father has implemented a plan for our happiness and progression. Because of this plan, everyone's ultimate potential is to become everything good, meaning to become perfect in every way. No matter your current circumstance and shortcomings, God has provided a way for you to progress. If you deeply want it, there is a way for you to become everything good. This is a beautiful truth.

Our existence is more than this mortal life. We existed before physical birth. We continue to exist after physical death. Our existence has purpose. We are on earth to experience, learn, and choose. We will travel Heavenly Father's path of happiness and progression as far as we choose to travel it, whether we realize what we are doing or not.

What more could a loving Heavenly Father give us than an opportunity to progress, if we so choose, until we become everything good?

Is this just sappy, feel-good prose? No. Mortal life does have a beautiful and ingenious underlying purpose.

How, then, do we progress to our ultimate potential? Our efforts certainly are needed, but there is more to Heavenly Father's plan than our efforts. He provides guidance, assistance, support, and more. His plan includes mercy and love, lifting us when we fail. He uses methods and ways that help us eternally, whether we recognize and understand them or not. Because of his plan, we can become more than the sum of our efforts. With God's "boosts", we can become full of love, absolutely pure, know all knowledge, have all abilities, feel all joy, and be all good. We can become complete, whole, perfect.

Our transformation can be like the changing of a cold, drizzly, drab predawn into a bright, clean, invigorating day —complete with warm sunshine and a vibrant rainbow. God is kind in giving us this opportunity to transform into a being more beautiful and complete than we currently are.

The potential to become everything good is not a pressure-laden trap demanding that we be flawless now. God is not mean. Heavenly Father does not pressure us like a competitive, judging society. Neither does our potential refer to a vague or mystical perfection that sounds nice but doesn't mean anything.

When someone understands that because of God's plan, they have a realistic opportunity to become everything good, that understanding stabilizes them. It helps them know who they are and their worth. It gives them purpose and hope. It frees them from the pressures of worldly successes and judgments.

The more an individual learns about Heavenly Father's plan, with the helps he provides, the more that individual realizes God has given them an amazing opportunity. This understanding frees them from the pressures of societal perfectionism. You do not have to be perfect to progress towards everything good. This is important to understand. You do not have to "perform perfectly" to progress towards everything good. You can have "flaws" and still progress.

You will probably make some unwise choices while on earth, but that doesn't mean your progression can't continue. Heavenly Father loves and values you. It is important to him that your opportunity to progress remains, despite poor decisions.

When you accept that you are loved, valued, and can in reality become everything good, this frees you from the shackles of self-doubt and low self-esteem. Accept this beautiful teaching. Even if you don't fully understand it you can accept it.

The Bible teaches our ultimate potential in plain text. Consider the following scripture about the purpose of scriptures; especially notice the teaching about our potential.

> "<u>All</u> <u>scripture</u> <u>is</u> <u>given</u> by inspiration of God, and is profitable <u>for</u> <u>doctrine</u>, <u>for</u> <u>reproof</u>, <u>for</u> <u>correction</u>, <u>for</u> <u>instruction</u> in righteousness:
>
> <u>That</u> <u>the</u> <u>man</u> [<u>woman</u>] <u>of</u> <u>God</u> <u>may</u> <u>be</u> <u>perfect</u>, <u>thoroughly</u> <u>furnished</u> <u>unto</u> <u>all</u> <u>good</u> <u>works</u>" (2 Timothy 3:16–17 KJV).

Studying, pondering, and living by the teachings within the scriptures draws us closer to God.

Scriptures instruct, inspire, enlighten, and correct us. Inspired by God, they help us become better individuals. God gave them to us to help us become more like him. He wants us to enjoy the happiness he enjoys.

As we learn Heavenly Father's way and live his way, we change, becoming better individuals, our knowledge grows, our abilities increase, and our capacity to receive expands. We become more like the Divine.

If we continue living in God's way, remaining willing to change and progress, then our ultimate potential becomes as the scripture said, "may be perfect, thoroughly furnished unto all good works".

Some people miss or don't understand this crowning message when they study the Bible. They might see a beautiful future, but only partially grasp their full potential. They miss the inspiring reality of their divine worth.

We came from a heavenly home where we were loved and valued. Now, we are like travelers visiting a distant land, experiencing new ideas that expand our horizons. But mortality is not our permanent home. It is a temporary place within Heavenly Father's plan, a place for us to learn and choose.

Because Heavenly Father loves us, there is more to our progression in mortality than our efforts to improve. Just as a mother helps her child in ways the child does not yet understand, so Heavenly Father helps us in ways we don't yet fully understand. He cares for and helps us in ways that impact us eternally for good.

Consider the "more-than-just-our-effort" helps alluded to in the following two scriptures.

> "And I will bring the blind by a way they knew not; I will lead them in paths that they have not known: I will make darkness light before them, and crooked things straight. These things will I do unto them, and not forsake them" (Isaiah 42:16 KJV).

God has the power to bless us beyond our efforts. Paths exist that we do not yet see. There are ways that we do not yet know. God uses methods we don't fully understand, changing darkness to light and crooked to straight. He will not forsake us.

> "To appoint unto them that mourn in Zion, to give unto them beauty for ashes, the oil of joy for mourning, the garment of praise for the spirit of heaviness; that they might be called trees of righteousness, the planting of the Lord, that he might be glorified" (Isaiah 61:3 KJV).

Within Heavenly Father's plan seemingly insignificant individuals (from a societal point of view), seeds that are dry and shriveled, people that mourn with heavy burdens or heavy sins, lives that are in ashes, can become stately, beautiful, fruitful trees, "the planting of the Lord", ashes to beauty, mourning to joy, heaviness to praise. We, each individual, can become a tree of righteousness.

This teaching is beautiful indeed. But is it true? Yes, it is true. You can know it is true by the means God provides. Jesus taught us an important way to learn and know truth.

> "But the Comforter, which is the Holy Ghost, whom the Father will send in my name, he shall teach you all things, and bring all things to your remembrance, whatsoever I have said unto you" (John 14:26 KJV).

The Holy Ghost teaches all things. You can learn from the Holy Ghost about your ultimate potential. Be aware of the thoughts, feelings, and peace God sends to you through the Holy Ghost. This special helper from God called the Holy Ghost, the Comforter, the Holy Spirit will teach and confirm truth to you.

Receive what Heavenly Father gives you via the Holy Ghost.

THE PLAN OF PROGRESSION AND HAPPINESS

We did not burst into existence at birth. We existed before this mortal life as spirit children of God. This is who we are. We came from God. We are related to him. He is the Father of our spirit, our Heavenly Father. He knows us. He loves us. He cares deeply about each one of us. Heavenly Father desires we become good like he is good. He wants us to have a fullness of joy. He established a way for us to become like him.

During our premortal, pre-earth existence, Heavenly Father presented his plan for our progression and happiness. The plan includes experience, agency, progression, salvation, and exaltation. Let's consider each of these items.

   • Experience: we need to experience to understand the things of God. We are on this earth having experiences, learning the differences between good and evil.

• Agency: God gives us agency. We choose for ourselves. No one else can choose for us. We are choosing the type of individual we are becoming.

• Progression: we can progress spiritually a step at a time, becoming better individuals as we learn and choose to be good.

• Salvation: the plan includes a savior. Heavenly Father knew we would make bad choices. We would sin. The sinless Savior has power to rectify our wrongs and change the eternal consequences of our sins. The Savior extends mercy to us. Because of him, we can continue along the path of progression and happiness.

• Exaltation: God can exalt us to a fullness of joy, a fullness of happiness, to everything good. He will not force us towards exaltation; everyone goes as far as they want.

We came from Heavenly Father.

When Heavenly Father told us his plan, Lucifer, one of Heavenly Father's spirit children, tried to change the plan to promote himself.

Lying about his intentions, Lucifer said he would "save" everyone. He argued to control our mortal experience and return everyone to Heavenly Father. In reality, Lucifer sought to aggrandize himself. He wanted to discard agency and rule over us. Lucifer wanted to take God's place. He did not want to become everything good. He wanted power, glory, and control.

Heavenly Father rejected Lucifer's alterations to his plan. After not getting his way, Lucifer's true intentions came forth. He rebelled against God, starting a war with Heavenly Father. He tried to persuade us to follow him. Some of Heavenly Father's spirit children did follow Lucifer, perhaps hoping to aggrandize themselves. The scriptures refer to this as the war in heaven.

> "And there was war in heaven: Michael [a servant of God] and his angels fought against the dragon [Lucifer]; and the dragon fought and his angels [the spirit children that followed Lucifer],
> And prevailed not; neither was their place found any more in heaven.
> And the great dragon was cast out, that old serpent, called the Devil, and Satan, which deceiveth the whole world: he was cast out into the earth, and his angels were cast out with him" (Revelation 12:7–9 KJV).

Lucifer and the spirits that followed him were cast out of Heavenly Father's presence. They chose to fight against God rather than follow the path of progression and happiness. Because of their choice, they do not have the same opportunities as we now have, to receive physical bodies and to learn from the experiences of mortal life. In open rebellion to God and everything good, in the very presence of God the Father, they chose to follow the path of evil. They are now the source of evil and temptation in the world. They continue fighting against God.

Satan tries to thwart God's plan. He still seeks to aggrandize himself. He seeks to control us. Mad that we chose Heavenly Father's plan and jealous of our opportunity to progress, he hates us. He desires to make us miserable.

Satan probably believes that for every person he persuades to do evil or to not believe in God, he thwarts God's plan, thereby showing that he is more powerful than God, glorifying himself. He is a liar. He lies to himself. He lies to others. Satan does not have all power; God has all power. Heavenly Father's plan will continue to its conclusion despite the efforts of Satan and the evil spirits that followed him.

Heavenly Father allows Satan to tempt us so that we can learn and choose between good and evil. But God will not allow Satan to thwart his plan. Anyone who wants to progress along Heavenly Father's plan of happiness may, despite Satan.

The fact that you were born, receiving a physical body to go along with your spiritual body, means that during the premortal existence, you sided with those wanting to continue progressing according to Heavenly Father's plan. You accepted Heavenly Father's choice of Jesus Christ as the Savior. You did not follow Lucifer. In Heavenly Father's presence, you chose God's way.

You are now on the earth in a school of opportunity, without memories of your premortal existence. Many influences entice you to choose evil, and many influences persuade you to choose good. The forces of evil are strong. But the forces of good are stronger, much stronger.

Mortality is a time for learning while not directly in Heavenly Father's presence. Your physical body allows you to have physical experiences. Through these experiences, your opportunities to learn increase. You can learn the difference between good actions and bad actions, the difference between serving others and being selfish, the difference between uplifting thoughts and degrading thoughts, the difference between acting upon helpful emotions or acting upon destructive emotions, the difference between holy feelings and evil feelings, the difference between righteous desires and evil desires.

You can learn the value of love, obedience, and self-control. You can learn and choose patterns of life that bring you happiness. Or you can learn and choose patterns of life that bring you misery. You feel the effects of your actions for good or for bad, enjoying or suffering the consequences of your actions.

Mortality is a time for choosing. You choose what you do and don't do. Other people's choices and actions can influence you. They may hurt or help you. But each individual chooses their own actions and reactions to the experiences of mortal life.

You are currently choosing between good and evil without "seeing" Heavenly Father. God does not force you to be good. Satan cannot force you to be evil. You choose the type of individual you become according to your desires. No one else chooses for you.

When stripped of all the facades mortal life contains, you will be the person you chose to be, seen for who you truly are, good, bad, or something in between. No matter what others do or don't do to you or for you, you decide the type of person you are because you decide how you act and react.

Heavenly Father loves you. Agency is one of his precious gifts to you, an opportunity to choose. This is fabulous.

However, the path of spiritual growth is not all pleasant. It has challenges. It is not always easy to be good. The path will be difficult at times. Mortal life can be quite harsh. Sometimes we aren't even sure of the "good thing to do" in a particular situation. We need help and guidance as we learn from our experiences.

Heavenly Father has not left us helpless. He provides assistance to help us learn, progress spiritually, and enjoy our time in mortality. However, he doesn't force his help on anyone. Each person chooses if they will accept and use his help.

Here are some of the "helps" Heavenly Father provides.

Each of the following helps can bless you in unique ways. Further, each help can also overlap with other helps for harmonious and powerful assistance.

- Parents, while imperfect, usually love, nurture, and teach newly arrived spirits the best they can. You can probably learn from your parents whether their example is good or bad.

- Your conscience guides and prompts you with a basic understanding of right and wrong. If you go against your conscience, you feel it within.

- Examples of love, kindness, and goodness exist all over the world, in every culture, among all people.

- Heavenly Father loves you unconditionally. You don't have to perform to be loved. You are loved. His love can comfort and strengthen you. When you feel his love it is powerful.

- God gives you commandments that gently guide you along the path of happiness. The commandments are understandable boundaries between good and evil.

- Prophets, sent by God, reveal and teach Heavenly Father's plan of happiness; they teach God's way of living; they call you to repentance and encourage you to obey the commandments.

• Scriptures allow you to study inspired messages from God. In them, you can learn about Heavenly Father's plan and the way to live. You can study other people's experiences of trying to live God's way.

• You can pray directly to Heavenly Father, seeking him, trusting him, thanking him, and asking him to guide you.

• The Holy Ghost prompts and guides you towards truth, testifies of truth so you can recognize it, and confirms truth to you as you accept it.

• The Holy Ghost also comforts you so that the injustices of mortal life do not overwhelm you.

• Heavenly Father provides a savior, Jesus Christ. The Savior helps you in ways that you cannot help yourself. He saves.

A useful truth to understand is that we continue to exist after this mortal life. Regardless of what you personally believe, you continue after mortality. You will die physically, yes; but that is not the end. Death ends our time in mortality and returns us to the spirit world. You still exist. When you accept this truth, it helps you keep your mortal experiences (which are temporary) in perspective.

At the time of physical death, your spirit separates from your physical body. Without the spirit, your physical body becomes lifeless and decays. Your spirit continues. Your intelligence remains active. That part of you that thinks and is aware, that part of you that likes and dislikes, that part of you that acts and reacts, that part of you that chooses, that part of you that is who you really are, being eternal, continues. You will have the same tendencies, desires, and aptitudes you developed while living on the earth. You'll be the same person after physical death as you were before.

God's plan continues. But do not assume that the next phase of the plan is a repeat of this phase.

The time to learn and choose between good and evil is now, during mortal life. The time to overcome evil tendencies is now. The time to develop your abilities to love and serve others is now. The next part of Heavenly Father's plan builds upon this phase. But it is not more of the same. Our great opportunity is now. Learn to be good now. Make the changes to become the person you truly want to be now.

Heavenly Father's plan includes resurrection. Resurrection is the reuniting of spirit and physical body, never to be separated again. After a time in the spirit world, you will be resurrected. Jesus Christ made your resurrection a reality through his resurrection. He conquered physical death and gives to all the gift of the resurrection.

Every person will be resurrected, the righteous, the wicked, the kind, the mean, the calm, the nervous, the extrovert, the introvert, the believer, the non-believer, those that die old, those that die young—everyone. Each spirit will rejoin with the physical body. It is a gift from the Savior.

Your resurrected body will not be exactly as you are now. You will no longer be subject to physical death. Physical deformities will not exist. The cumbersomeness and tiredness associated with the physical body will not exist. Your ability to move and do will increase. (Regardless of how you feel about your physical body, you will like your resurrected body.) Most importantly, your resurrected body will have the powers of divine glory you are capable of receiving based on the person you became.

Heavenly Father's plan includes a day of reckoning, a time of spiritual accounting. The weighing of your choices within the opportunities and circumstances of your life. This "judgment" mercifully and lovingly designates a "place" for you that fits who you desired to become. Your "judgment" is not God condemning you. It is God sharing with you whatever amount of eternal glory and happiness your resurrected self can handle.

Some people think of God as a condemning god. This is not true. Our Heavenly Father is a loving, sharing being. He will share with us everything good that we can receive. If we are not capable of receiving more, it will be because of our own choices, not because God is mean. He is not mean. Do not believe teachers or preachers that try to scare with threats of a condemning God.

Because God loves you, you will eternally enjoy the degree of happiness that the type of individual you became can receive. God loves all his children. He will give each of us the best we can receive. Each person will be accountable for their sins, but God will give us the best we can receive.

Different levels of happiness and ability await based upon our choices and desires. If someone sincerely desires to be good, even if that person doesn't currently know about

Heavenly Father's plan or Jesus Christ, but desires to be loving, pure, and selfless, etc., that person will strive to live like that; then, with the help of the Savior (recognized or not), that person will eternally enjoy the opportunities, abilities, and happiness associated with being that type of person.

Similarly, if a person desires to be evil, to lie, to hate, to be selfish, to promulgate pain, or get revenge, etc., then that person will choose to live like that, and will eternally suffer the self-imposed hindrances, underdeveloped abilities, and lack of happiness that flows from being that type of person.

- - - - - - - - - - - - - - - - - - -

Equal opportunities during mortality do not exist for everyone. Some parents neglect or abuse their children. People are ignored, discounted, or abused as adults. Some people live and suffer during times of war. Many people struggle to get life's necessities or don't have opportunities for education and employment. Some people may not learn of Heavenly Father's Plan of Happiness. Many people do not know of the spiritual helps available.

People live different lengths of time. Infants die. People suffer because of the evil choices of others. Natural disasters affect some people and completely miss other people. Inequalities, deprivations, and misfortunes could be listed at length. With so much inequality on earth, how can Heavenly Father's plan be fair, yet allow those who choose to be evil, to, in fact, be evil?

Heavenly Father's plan is all-encompassing. Through the entire plan, God will level the injustices and inequalities of mortal life. Four key factors ensure eternal equity, justice, mercy, and love for all.

First, our all-knowing, all-powerful Heavenly Father controls all factors. Nothing blindsides him. Just because we may not see or understand does not mean God does not see or understand. He is in control.

> "<u>For</u> <u>my</u> <u>thoughts</u> <u>are</u> <u>not</u> <u>your</u> <u>thoughts</u>, neither are your ways my ways, saith the Lord.
> For as the heavens are higher than the earth, so are <u>my</u> <u>ways</u> <u>higher</u> <u>than</u> <u>your</u> <u>ways</u>, and my thoughts than your thoughts" (Isaiah 55:8–9 KJV).

Second, this earth life is only part of Heavenly Father's plan, not the entire plan. We existed before mortality. We continue to exist after physical death. Mortality is of short duration compared to the reality that we exist forever.

Third, everyone becomes as good as they desire without being forced or limited. The evil actions of others certainly impact us, just as the good actions of others impact us, but they do not decide who we are or our destiny. We decide. All the inequalities on earth may limit our earthly opportunities, but they do not determine our eternal opportunities. We, not someone else, decide how good we strive to be and eventually will become.

Fourth, Jesus Christ has power to heal all wounds, make right all injustices, and correct all wrongs. His power to heal is physical, emotional, mental, spiritual—total, all-encompassing.

He is omnipotent. If you suffer at the hands of others, you will be healed. You will be comforted and loved deeply. Right now, evil can be evil. But evil will not always have the power to hurt you. The only way evil will be part of your eternity is if you yourself choose to be evil.

Your kind, loving, all-powerful, all-knowing Heavenly Father will, through the course of his entire plan, be fair and kind to you. Heavenly Father and Jesus Christ know you as an individual. All the conditions, all the extremities, all the injustices, all the special circumstances, all the opportunities or lack of opportunities during your mortal life will be fully considered in the balance of their omniscience and love. God will be fair to you.

> "Justice and judgment are the habitation of thy throne: mercy and truth shall go before thy face" (Psalm 89:14 KJV).

> "...the judgments of the Lord are true and righteous..." (Psalm 19:9 KJV).

> "...just and true are thy ways, thou King of saints" (Revelation 15:3 KJV).

Heavenly Father will not forget or slight anyone. His plan is complete. You are his spirit daughter or son. He loves you unconditionally. God will not neglect, overlook, or forget you.

BIBLICAL

TEACHINGS

OF

OUR

POTENTIAL

Follow Jesus

We begin to understand our eternal potential through the invitation to follow Jesus Christ.

Jesus Christ knows the way to live. During his earthly life, he lived untangled by sin. He lived a perfect life. He was not self-serving or acting good for show. He was good. He is good. He knows how to live. He asks us to follow him.

> "And he said to them all, If any man [woman] will come after me, let him [her] deny himself [herself], and take up his [her] cross daily, and <u>follow</u> <u>me</u>" (Luke 9:23 KJV).

The Savior said, "follow me." Be like me. Deny yourself the easy path of sin. Rise above evil. Follow and become like me.

Striving to be like Jesus is the best way to live. It is the path of lasting happiness. But following Jesus can be difficult.

Disciples of Christ may have to endure ridicule as they strive to be good. They may have to forgo worldly recognition or do without some enjoyable aspects of life. People may misunderstand or reject them. Certainly, followers of Christ must do the arduous tasks of controlling and tempering self. Following Christ is not always easy.

> "And he [she] that taketh not his [her] cross, and followeth after me, is not worthy of me" (Matthew 10:38 KJV).

To truly follow Christ, we need to endure whatever hardships the world throws at us for following him. But easy or not, every effort we make to follow Jesus is worth it. We become more like him as we strive to follow him.

You are wise when you live according to the Savior's teachings.

> "Therefore whosoever heareth these sayings of mine, and doeth them, I will liken him [her] unto a wise man [woman], which built his [her] house upon a rock" (Matthew 7:24 KJV).

You build your character on a sure foundation when you hear Christ's teachings and do them. You are wise when you strive to do as he does, to act and react as he acts and reacts.

It is good to follow Jesus.

But Satan mocks God and strives to lead people astray. He entices people with pleasure, status, wealth, power, possessions, praise, glitter, anything that will lead people away from God. He and the evil spirits that follow him twist perceptions to make good appear evil and evil appear good. They want to deceive you. They seek for you to be evil, not because they care about you, but because they fight against God. They mock Heavenly Father, Jesus Christ, and the plan of happiness.

With Satan fighting against us, with all the temptations, distractions, and encumbrances available, an interesting question to consider is: how far can a person, in reality, follow Jesus?

Is it realistic to say we can follow Jesus to everything good? Can we follow him to perfection? Or must we stop somewhere along the way?

We may understand that we become better versions of ourselves when we sincerely strive to live by Jesus's teachings, but to what end? What is the real purpose the Savior asks us to follow him? How far can we, in reality, follow him? How perfect can we become? Often, our individual wisdom seems merely sufficient to recognize that we need to change, much less to follow the Savior flawlessly.

So, with our weaknesses, our sins, and our flawed following, how far can we travel the path of righteousness?

Through Jesus's grace, mercy, and atoning sacrifice, he can turn you into someone better than you currently are. Yes, of course, he can; but again, to what end? With Jesus's strength, his knowledge, his guidance, his teaching, his redeeming and cleansing power, his infinite atonement for sin, what is your ultimate potential? Is it true that you can someday become perfect, everything good?

Thoughtfully consider Jesus's command:

> "<u>Be</u> ye therefore <u>perfect</u>, <u>even</u> <u>as</u> <u>your</u> <u>Father</u> which is <u>in</u> <u>heaven</u> <u>is</u> <u>per-</u> <u>fect</u>" (Matthew 5:48 KJV).

Be perfect, become perfect, even as your Heavenly Father is perfect. Does the Savior mean what he said? Perhaps he simply meant to be a nice person; try to be perfect, but you won't really make it. Perhaps his words are thoughtless speech sounding nice but not meaning what they say. That is nonsense.

The Savior meant what he said. He knows how far you can travel the pathway of righteousness, even with your current imperfect status. He knows your true potential.

He atoned for your sins so that you could repent and overcome them. He provides means so you will not have to be stopped in your progression. He knows what he commanded you to become. He knows your potential.

We have a great opportunity. We can choose to follow the Savior, strive to obey his commandments with sincere intent, repent of sins when needed, and continue despite hardships and setbacks. As we persist in following Christ, eventually we will become complete, whole, perfect like our Father in Heaven. We can follow the Savior to the pinnacle of everything good.

> "Jesus saith unto him, I am the way,
> the truth, and the life: no man [woman]
> cometh unto the Father, but by me" (John
> 14:6 KJV).

Jesus is the way to the Father. He is eager to lead you to all that is good. He has the power, knowledge, and right to lead you to all the perfection of our Father in Heaven. You decide if you follow him, and you decide how sincerely you put forth effort to follow him.

- - - - - - - - - - - - - - - - - - -

A caution is in order. Please understand that the command to be perfect is not the "perfectionism" exhibited by people in a competitive society who are never satisfied with themselves, their accomplishments, or their improvement. Do not put worldly connotations on God's uplifting commands.

The Savior's command to be perfect, when understood within the light of Heavenly Father's plan, frees people, not burdens them. It opens opportunities, not closes. It uplifts, not discourages. Follow Jesus and experience increasing capacity, expanding opportunities, and deepening peace. Wonderful things await your spiritual discovery as you follow Christ.

The commandments, including the commandment to be perfect, open a greater world. As you strive to be good, you will feel spiritually healing balms and spiritually cleansing burnings. You will receive ever greater understanding and ennobling powers. Opportunities will open and expand for you. You will grow spiritually, becoming more like Heavenly Father.

Allow yourself to progress by accepting yourself with whatever spiritual condition you currently have. Don't demand yourself to perform perfectly. Be kind to yourself and allow yourself to improve by believing and following Jesus. Apply his teachings to your life. Sincerely, strive to be good. You will progress.

Understand that with the Savior you can overcome anything wrong within yourself and someday become everything good. With his power, you can bring forth spiritual fruit that alone you could not produce. Jesus said,

> "Abide in me, and I in you. As the branch cannot bear fruit of itself, except it abide in the vine: no more can ye, except ye <u>abide</u> <u>in</u> <u>me</u>.
>
> I am the vine, ye are the branches: He that abideth in me, and I in him, <u>the</u> <u>same</u> <u>bringeth</u> <u>forth</u> <u>much</u> <u>fruit</u>: for without me ye can do nothing" (John 15:4–5 KJV).

With Jesus, we can bear much fruit, the fruit of our full potential.

The invitation to follow Jesus is an invitation to become. Mercifully, it does not include a requirement to live flawlessly now. But as we follow the Savior, living as he lives, our eternal self blossoms and takes shape.

Follow Jesus Christ as far as it is possible to follow him. Do not deny blessings to yourself by stopping your efforts to follow him. Follow him and continue following him, striving to live the way he taught. Follow him to everything good.

Follow the Savior. He is the path to everything good.

SALVATION

When we understand what it means to be saved, we see more clearly our eternal potential.

Jesus is the Savior. A heavenly messenger at the time of Jesus's birth declared,

> "And she shall bring forth a son, and thou shalt call his name <u>JESUS</u>: for he <u>shall</u> <u>save</u> <u>his</u> <u>people</u> <u>from</u> <u>their</u> <u>sins</u>" (Matthew 1:21 KJV).

Jesus has the power to save people from sin.

Sin affects us. Choosing to sin has consequences. All sins impede our spiritual progress. Sin darkens our mind, clouds our judgment, and makes it more difficult for us to discern between truth and error. Some sins damage our physical well-being. All sins damage our spiritual well-being. Participating in sin causes us to become spiritually unclean. Regularly participating in sin causes us to feel dejected and doubt our worth. Sin leads us away from Heavenly Father. Choosing sin makes us spiritually unfit for the kingdom of God.

We all have sinned and should not deceive ourselves.

> "For all have sinned, and come short
> of the glory of God" (Romans 3:23 KJV).

All of us are short of God's glory, of God's perfection. We all have sinned and have a predicament. We want to be better than we currently are, becoming more like Heavenly Father, but our sins hinder our progress. We need to be saved from our sins.

The Savior has power to save us. What does this mean? It means that Jesus has the power to cleanse our souls, making us worthy of spiritual blessings. Jesus can remove spiritual blockades so that we can continue to progress spiritually. It means that he can take us from bad to good.

We need to repent of our sins and strive to obey God's commandments, but we can't spiritually cleanse ourselves. The Savior cleanses us. Sincere repentance is how we ask for and receive the saving, cleansing grace of the Savior.

We may not fully understand how Jesus cleanses our souls, but we can understand the concept and accept his role as Savior.

Similar to the question of how far can you follow the Savior, is how far can the Savior save you? How removed from evil can the Savior take you? How pure can he cause you to become? What amount of knowledge can he teach you?

How much joy and happiness can he give you? How far can the Savior save you?

A verse from the writings of the Apostle Paul teaches what the believer already feels within.

> "Wherefore <u>he</u> <u>is</u> <u>able</u> <u>also</u> <u>to</u> <u>save</u> <u>them</u> <u>to</u> <u>the</u> <u>uttermost</u> that come unto God by him, seeing he ever liveth to make intercession for them" (Hebrews 7:25 KJV).

For those that "come unto God by him," Jesus saves them to the uttermost. He saves them completely, thoroughly.

Jesus can take you from evil, misery, and sin and lead you to Heavenly Father, joy, and everything good. He can cleanse your soul from the stains of sin. He can save you from the long-term effects and consequences of sin, from misery to happiness, from ignorance to knowledge, from filthiness to purity, from darkness to light, from spiritual death to spiritual life, from behaving similar to Satan to becoming similar to God, from evil to everything good.

Jesus can do for you that which you cannot do for yourself

The Savior has the ability; he has the power to save you to the uttermost, without limit. No matter what you have done he can cleanse you. Jesus is the Master Healer, the healer of the spirit, as well as the physical body.

> "Come now, and let us reason to-gether, saith the Lord: <u>though your sins be as scarlet, they shall be as white as snow</u>; though they be red like crimson, they shall be as wool" (Isaiah 1:18 KJV).

The Savior can do for you that which you cannot do for yourself.

Even though we all have sinned and are not worthy of God's glory, we can change. Because of Jesus Christ, we can become worthy. Consider the Savior's redeeming and purifying power.

> "Who gave himself for us, <u>that he might redeem us from all iniquity, and purify</u> unto himself <u>a peculiar people, zealous of good works</u>" (Titus 2:14 KJV).

He can redeem us from all iniquity. He can purify us. We can become a pure people, a people zealous of good works.

- -

The Law of Moses, in the Old Testament, foreshadowed the Savior's atonement for sin. The animal sacrifices of that law symbolically taught of the coming sacrifice of the Savior. The Savior's sacrifice, the sacrifice of the Son of God, the

Lamb of God, would satisfy the demands of eternal justice and extend mercy to the repentant sinner.

God gave the Law of Moses to teach the people about the coming Messiah. It is through the Messiah that salvation is possible.

There are many symbols within the Law of Moses. The Law itself was a symbol of good things to come.

> "For the law having a shadow of good things to come, and not the very image of the things, can never with those sacrifices which they offered year by year continually make the comers thereunto perfect" (Hebrews 10:1 KJV).

The Law of Moses, with its animal sacrifices, could not make people perfect; but, the Law looked forward to the sacrifice of the Savior, and his sacrifice, Jesus's atonement for sin, can make people perfect.

> "By the which will we are sanctified through the offering of the body of Jesus Christ once for all...
>
> For by one offering he hath perfected for ever them that are sanctified.
>
> Whereof the Holy Ghost also is a witness to us..." (Hebrews 10:10,14–15 KJV).

Through Jesus's atonement for our sins, we can become perfect. He can strengthen us to overcome all evil. He can help us progress until we partake of all good. Through sanctifying us, Jesus perfects us.

The scripture just quoted teaches that the Holy Ghost witnesses to us the truth of these things. Be aware of your feelings, your enlightened thoughts, and the messages Heavenly Father sends to you as the Holy Ghost communicates with your spirit. Don't deny or ignore the witnesses God sends to you via the Holy Ghost.

The Savior has atoned for your sins, but he does not force you to accept his gifts. The question becomes, how far are you willing to be saved? Are you willing to repent and forsake your sins? Are you willing to accept his saving grace?

Accept Jesus. Believe Him. Our efforts, like ingredients in a simmering soup, when mixed with his power and grace, become a delicious, satisfying dish. Are you willing to be saved "to the uttermost"?

HEIRS AND JOINT HEIRS

The promise of becoming an heir of God and joint heir with Christ teaches our eternal potential.

Remember who you are and from whom you came. You came from God. You are his spirit child. He is your Heavenly Father. All the beliefs or lack of beliefs that have come and gone through the years of humanity's earthly existence do not change this simple truth: you came from God. He is your Heavenly Father.

> "Furthermore we have had fathers of our flesh which corrected us, and we gave them reverence: shall we not much rather be in subjection unto the <u>Father</u> <u>of</u> <u>spirits</u>, and live" (Hebrews 12:9 KJV).

We have an earthly father (that corrects us). In addition, we have a father of our spirit (whom we should reverence and receive correction from). This father is God, our Heavenly Father. Every human being has divinity in them. Because we

are from heavenly parents, we have intrinsic worth and
potential.

A verse in Genesis (the first book and first chapter of the
Bible) teaches our relationship with God.

> "So <u>God</u> <u>created</u> <u>man</u> [woman] <u>in</u> <u>his</u>
> <u>own</u> <u>image</u>, in the image of God created he
> him [them]; male and female created he
> them" (Genesis 1:27 KJV).

God created us in his image. He is the Father. We are the
children. God is not an essence, a force, nor an idea. He is
not something completely different from us; a better way to
say this is, we are not completely different from him.

There are many philosophies about God. Do not believe
false teachings that change the simple and powerful truth
that God is our Heavenly Father into some complex relationship between us and him.

> "For in him we live, and move, and
> have our being; as certain also of your own
> poets have said, For <u>we</u> <u>are</u> <u>also</u> <u>his</u> <u>off-</u>
> <u>spring</u>.
> Forasmuch then as we are the off-
> spring of God, we ought not to think that
> the Godhead is like unto gold, or silver, or
> stone, graven by art and man's de-
> vice" (Acts 17:28-29 KJV).

We are the offspring of God, his spirit children. Do not
think that God is an idea manufactured by humans to serve

human purposes. Neither believe that God is an idol made by human hands, nor that God is an intangible force or essence. Heavenly Father is real. We are his spirit offspring, created in his image. We may not now understand the details, but our spirit comes from divine parents.

The Holy Spirit will testify of this truth to your spirit.

> "<u>The</u> <u>Spirit</u> <u>itself</u> <u>beareth</u> <u>witness</u> <u>with</u> <u>our</u> <u>spirit,</u> <u>that</u> <u>we</u> <u>are</u> <u>the</u> <u>children</u> <u>of</u> <u>God</u>" (Romans 8:16 KJV).

Receive this truth. Do not dismiss it, complicate it, or harden your heart and drive it away. God will not force knowledge upon you, but you can know through the Holy Spirit that you came from him.

All of God's creations are important; humans, however, are his offspring. Since we came from God, we have tremendous potential, potential to inherit the things of God.

> "And <u>if</u> <u>children,</u> <u>then</u> <u>heirs;</u> <u>heirs</u> <u>of</u> <u>God,</u> <u>and</u> <u>joint-heirs</u> <u>with</u> <u>Christ</u>; if so be that we suffer with him, that we may be also glorified together" (Romans 8:17 KJV).

Our potential taught by this scripture refers to a grandeur we humans don't fully understand. It teaches that we, the children of God, can become heirs of God and joint heirs with Christ. This is one of the most glorious teachings ever taught. It is a truth Satan does not want us to understand.

On this earth, we are as little children ignorant of many things. We are learning, making mistakes, and sometimes sinning. We do not live perfect lives. Yet, our wise Heavenly Father provided a savior. Because of Jesus Christ, we can repent and become spiritually clean. We can learn to choose more wisely. With Christ, we can become the type of child that will be an heir of God and a joint heir with Christ.

We do not automatically inherit all the goodness that is Heavenly Father's just because we are his spirit children. Not everyone will become heirs in the fullest sense. Sin creates barriers that hinder our progress. But the Savior can remove these barriers.

> "But <u>as</u> <u>many</u> <u>as</u> <u>received</u> <u>him</u>, <u>to</u> <u>them</u> <u>gave</u> <u>he</u> <u>power</u> <u>to</u> <u>become</u> <u>the</u> <u>sons</u> <u>[daughters]</u> <u>of</u> <u>God</u>, even to them that believe on his name" (John 1:12 KJV).

If you choose to receive and believe in Christ, he has the power to change you—with you becoming a daughter or son of God in a special sense. You can become a child that will become an heir of God and a joint heir with Christ.

Consider the symbolism of being born again. Jesus taught,

> "...Verily, verily, I say unto thee, <u>Except</u> <u>a</u> <u>man</u> <u>[woman]</u> <u>be</u> <u>born</u> <u>again</u>, <u>he</u> <u>[she]</u> <u>cannot</u> <u>see</u> <u>the</u> <u>kingdom</u> <u>of</u> <u>God</u>" (John 3:3 KJV).

We must be "born again" to see the kingdom of God. Christian churches commonly teach this. What does it mean?

Jesus continued.

> "...Verily, verily, I say unto thee, <u>Except</u> <u>a</u> <u>man</u> [woman] <u>be</u> <u>born</u> <u>of</u> <u>water</u> <u>and</u> <u>of</u> <u>the</u> <u>spirit,</u> <u>he</u> [she] <u>cannot</u> <u>enter</u> <u>into</u> <u>the</u> <u>kingdom</u> <u>of</u> <u>God</u>" (John 3:5 KJV).

The ordinance of baptism is to be "born of water". It symbolizes the coming forth of a new life, a spiritually unclean soul becoming cleansed of sin and set on a new and better path. It represents a child of God that covenants to live according to the example of Jesus Christ.

(Jesus cleanses us, not the water.)

Being "born of the spirit" is to receive the Holy Ghost, to be refined, purified, and sanctified by his influence, as if by fire. This wonderful gift is given to those baptized by God's authority and will continue with them on their new and better path.

Because of the Savior's atonement, through the baptism of water and the purifying of the Holy Ghost, we become clean. If we continue on this path, we become worthy daughters and sons of God that will inherit a place within the Father's kingdom.

> "<u>Wherefore</u> <u>thou</u> <u>art</u> <u>no</u> <u>more</u> <u>a</u> <u>servant,</u> <u>but</u> <u>a</u> <u>son</u> [daughter]; <u>and</u> <u>if</u> <u>a</u> <u>son</u> [daughter], <u>then</u> <u>an</u> <u>heir</u> <u>of</u> <u>God</u> <u>through</u> <u>Christ</u>" (Galatians 4:7 KJV).

Consider what it means to be an heir of God and a joint heir with Christ.

> "To him [her] that overcometh will I grant to sit with me in my throne, even as I also overcame, and am set down with my Father in his throne.
>
> He that hath an ear, let him hear what the Spirit saith unto the churches" (Revelation 3:21-22 KJV).

To be an heir of God and a joint heir with Christ means we overcome evil and become worthy of living with Christ in the Father's kingdom. We sit with Christ on his throne, just as Christ overcame evil and sits on the Father's throne.

This scripture teaches much of Heavenly Father's plan. It teaches that we must overcome evil. This implies action, effort on our part. We must exert effort to overcome evil; we must repent and strive to live by God's commandments. However, by our own efforts, we do not earn the right to sit on Christ's throne. He grants that to us. This is his grace, his mercy, his atonement for our sins. Then, we become part of Christ's reign just as he became part of the Father's reign.

This scripture concludes with, "hear what the Spirit saith". Some people will hear. Some people will not hear. Each person chooses whether or not they will believe. We are not forced. We either engage our progression or limit it by what we choose to believe.

Believe Christ. Strive to follow him. Let righteous actions and efforts refine you. Embrace goodness. You are a spirit child of God. You have a divine origin and a divine potential. Because of Jesus Christ, you can become the type of child that will become an heir of God and a joint heir with Christ.

THE FATHER, THE SON, AND US

The relationships of God the Father to us, God the Father to God the Son, and God the Son to us teach our eternal potential—with the relationship between Heavenly Father and Jesus Christ serving as a parallel to the relationship between Jesus Christ and us.

First, consider the relationship between Heavenly Father and Jesus Christ. Jesus is the only begotten son of Heavenly Father in the flesh. Jesus's relationship with Heavenly Father differs from ours. Jesus did not have an earthly father as we do.

> "For <u>God</u> so loved the world, that he <u>gave</u> <u>his</u> <u>only</u> <u>begotten</u> <u>Son</u>, <u>that</u> <u>whoso-</u><u>ever</u> <u>believeth</u> <u>in</u> <u>him</u> <u>should</u> <u>not</u> <u>perish,</u> <u>but</u> <u>have</u> <u>everlasting</u> <u>life</u>" (John 3:16 KJV).

This special sonship gave Jesus the power that whosoever believes in him should not perish but could have everlasting life.

Here is more about their relationship.

> "Then answered Jesus and said unto them, Verily, verily, I say unto you, The Son can do nothing of himself, but what he seeth the Father do: for what things soever he doeth, these also doeth the Son likewise" (John 5:19 KJV).

The Son does those things that he sees the Father do. Jesus lives as the Father lives. Heavenly Father is Jesus's perfect example. Jesus chose to obey and follow his father.

> "And he that sent me is with me: the Father hath not left me alone; for I do always those things that please him" (John 8:29 KJV).

> "Then said Jesus unto them, When ye have lifted up the Son of man, then shall ye know that I am he, and that I do nothing of myself; but as my Father hath taught me, I speak these things" (John 8:28 KJV).

The Father taught the Son, and the Son received the teachings. The Son does only those things that please the Father. He lives the way the Father taught him. Accordingly, Heavenly Father gave Jesus everything.

> "The Father loveth the Son, and hath given all things into his hand" (John 3:35 KJV).

The Father loves the Son and gave all things to him. Jesus has all knowledge, all power, and all glory. He is God the Son.

Now consider the relationship between Jesus and us.

> "Wherefore, come out from among them, and be ye separate, saith the Lord, and touch not the unclean thing; and I will receive you.
> And will be a Father unto you, and ye shall be my sons and daughters, saith the Lord Almighty" (2 Corinthians 6:17–18 KJV).

If you follow Jesus as Jesus followed the Father, Jesus symbolically becomes a Father to you. He teaches you how to live. He teaches you as the Father taught him.

The parallel continues.

> "He [she] that overcometh shall inherit all things; and I will be his [her] God, and he shall be my son [daughter]" (Revelation 21:7 KJV).

If we overcome evil, we will inherit all things. Jesus will be our God. This analogy states that we become the Savior's children. He is our God, similar to Heavenly Father, and he will give us all things.

The analogy reminds us that Jesus is divine as it teaches us he is the way to everything that is good.

Relationships

Heavenly Father is:
Father of Jesus's Spirit and Physical Body
Father of Our Spirit

Heavenly Father is:
Jesus's God
Our God

- - - - - - - - - - - - - -

Because Heavenly Father appointed Jesus
as the Savior, Jesus Christ is:
As a Father to Us
God to Us

The Savior wants to give us all things just as he received all things from the Father.

> "<u>Ask</u>, and it shall be given you; <u>seek</u>, and ye shall find; <u>knock</u>, and it shall be opened unto you:
> For <u>every</u> <u>one</u> <u>that</u> <u>asketh</u> <u>receiveth</u>; and <u>he</u> [<u>she</u>] <u>that</u> <u>seeketh</u> <u>findeth</u>; and <u>to</u> <u>him</u> [<u>her</u>] <u>that</u> <u>knocketh</u> <u>it</u> <u>shall</u> <u>be</u> <u>opened</u>" (Matthew 7:7–8 KJV).

Is there any limit to what you can learn or receive? Ask, it shall be given to you; seek, ye shall find; knock, it shall be opened to you. There is no limit.

Heavenly Father and Jesus eagerly give you everything as you are able and willing to receive. We become the cause of our limits when we choose to stop seeking, to stop knocking, to stop asking.

When we accept and live by truth, our capacity to learn and understand increases. We become capable of receiving more truths.

Note the promise in the following words from Jesus.

> "If any man [woman] have ears to hear, let him [her] hear.
> And he said unto them, Take heed what ye hear: with what measure ye mete, it shall be measured to you: and <u>unto you that hear shall more be given</u>" (Mark 4: 23–24 KJV).

The promise "unto you that hear shall more be given" reveals a key to becoming like Heavenly Father. As we accept and live by truth, God will give us more truth. It is not required to understand all of God's ways at once. The key is to accept the truth before us, and he will open opportunities to learn more of his ways.

If we reject truth, we become stagnant, like pond water with no place to go. If we persist in rejecting truth, our mind darkens.

If we are willing to learn, we can learn. We learn a little at a time. But that which we learn enables us to learn more. We build on our knowledge.

> "Whom shall he teach knowledge? and whom shall he make to understand doctrine? them that are weaned from the milk, and drawn from the breasts.
>
> For precept must be upon precept, precept upon precept: line upon line, line upon line; here a little, and there a little" (Isaiah 28:9–10 KJV).

We do not understand all of God's ways at once. But as we accept and live by truth, we gain more knowledge and power, our capacity increases, and our understanding of God expands.

If we continue on this path, eventually we will become like Jesus Christ and like Heavenly Father.

> "According as his divine power hath given unto us all things that pertain unto life and godliness, through the knowledge of him that hath called us to glory and virtue" (2 Peter 1:3 KJV).

We can receive all things that pertain to life and all things that pertain to godliness. This scripture teaches we have been called to glory and virtue through the knowledge of Christ.

Let us learn about Christ and be persistent in following him. Then, just as Christ received all things from Heavenly Father, we will receive all things from the Savior.

The Holy Ghost will guide us if we allow him.

> "Howbeit when he, <u>the Spirit of truth</u>, is come, <u>he will guide you into all truth</u>: for he shall not speak of himself; but whatsoever he shall hear, that shall he speak: and he will shew you things to come" (John 16:13 KJV).

The Spirit of truth, the Holy Spirit, the Holy Ghost will guide you to all truth. With the Holy Ghost's promptings, feelings, inspirations, comforts, or peace, you can discern truth from the myriad of religious and secular teachings existing in the world. Be aware of your feelings and thoughts. Take care to not reject the guidance from this special guide. Receive his witness of truth.

BECOME ONE

The invitation to become one with Divinity teaches our eternal potential. Jesus said,

> "I and my Father are one" (John 10:30 KJV).

Heavenly Father and Jesus Christ are one in perfection. They are two separate individuals: one is God the Father, and the other is God the Son. Yet they are completely one in purpose. Both are perfect. They work seamlessly together for our salvation and exaltation.

The Father has all knowledge; Jesus has all knowledge. The Father has all power; Jesus has all power. The Father is kind and merciful; Jesus is kind and merciful. The Father is pure and everything good; Jesus is pure and everything good. The Father is perfect; the Son is perfect.

They are two distinct individuals, yet one in perfection. They are one in purpose, with the Son doing the will of the Father.

Some people who heard Jesus say that he and his father were one accused him of blasphemy and tried to stone him (see John 10). They felt he was trying to make himself God. This is a very interesting accusation since Jesus Christ is the very individual who created the earth under the Father's direction. He is Jehovah, the great I Am of the Old Testament. He is God the Son who condescended to live on earth. He is the only begotten Son of the Father. He is the Savior. Yet these people tried to stone him because they thought he blasphemed.

Jesus responded to them by quoting a scripture and asking them a question.

> "Jesus answered them, <u>Is</u> <u>it</u> <u>not</u> <u>written</u> <u>in</u> <u>your</u> <u>law</u>, I said, <u>Ye</u> <u>are</u> <u>gods</u>?
> If <u>he</u> <u>called</u> <u>them</u> <u>gods</u>, unto whom the word of God came, and the scripture cannot be broken;
> <u>Say</u> <u>ye</u> of him, whom the Father hath sanctified, and sent into the world, <u>Thou</u> <u>blasphemest</u>; <u>because</u> <u>I</u> <u>said</u>, <u>I</u> <u>am</u> <u>the</u> <u>Son</u> <u>of</u> <u>God</u>" (John 10:34–36 KJV).

Jesus quoted a scripture that referred to the people to whom the word of God came as "gods". This scripture might be difficult to understand because we know humans are not "gods".

However, the principle Jesus taught isn't that complicated. It is this: if the person to whom the word of God came is someone special, then he who gave the message is truly someone greater.

Jesus, Jehovah, the God of the Old Testament who gave the words of scripture to the Old Testament prophets, is indeed greater than the prophets who received it. It was nonsense to accuse Jesus of blaspheming. He was and is who he claimed to be.

Jesus said to those people that wanted to kill him:

> "If I do not the works of my Father, believe me not.
> But if I do, though ye believe not me, believe the works: that ye may know, and believe, that the Father is in me, and I in him" (John 10:37–38 KJV).

Jesus does the works of the Father. He is in the Father and the Father is in him. They are one. They are two separate individuals, but one in goodness, one in purpose, one in perfection. They are alike.

Now consider this scripture about us.

> "Let this mind be in you, which was also in Christ Jesus:
> Who, being in the form of God, thought it not robbery to be equal with God" (Philippians 2:5–6 KJV).

Let this mind be in you, which was also in Christ Jesus—think the way the Savior thinks. Understand that Jesus's being "equal with God" does not rob God, does not take away from God the Father. When Jesus received all things from the Father, it was not robbery, because Heavenly Father gave all things to Jesus. The Father remains who he is. He retains his power, his authority, his knowledge, his goodness, his perfection, his Godhood, his position as God the Father.

Likewise, as we receive from deity, we are not robbing God. When Heavenly Father and Jesus give to us, it does not diminish what they have or who they are.

They want us to become like them. They want to share everything good with us. Jesus wants us to become one with the Father, just as he is one with Heavenly Father. Listen to the words of Jesus's prayer to the Father.

> "Neither pray I for these alone, but for them also that shall believe on me through their word;
>
> That they all may be one; as thou Father, art in me, and I in thee, <u>that they also may be one in us</u>: that the world may believe that thou hast sent me.
>
> And the glory which thou gavest me I have given them; that they may be one, even as we are one:
>
> <u>I in them, and thou in me, that they may be made perfect in one</u>; and that the world may know that thou hast sent me, and hast loved them, as thou hast loved me" (John 17:20–23 KJV).

We can be "made perfect in one" with the Father and with the Son, just as Jesus became one with the Father. We are distinct individuals. Heavenly Father is distinct. Jesus is distinct.

Heavenly Father and Jesus Christ
want us to become one with them.

Yet, we can become one with them as they are one.

Understand that becoming one with God does not mean you lessen or rob God. Neither does it mean you put yourself above God.

Jesus wants you to become like him. This does not mean you take his place. You do not become the Savior. Neither do you become God the Father. You do not become or replace God. Heavenly Father remains who he is. Jesus Christ remains who he is. You remain who you are, a child of God. You simply progress until you become like them, one with them.

Is it blasphemous to want to become one with the Father and with Jesus? Is it blasphemous to say that you can ultimately become perfect? Satan tries to persuade people to think it is blasphemous, a tactic that allows those thus hoodwinked to appear to love God but stops their progression. Stops them from reaching their full potential.

Satan wants to control and reign over you. He might try to deceive you into thinking that believing you can become one with the Father and Jesus is blasphemous, an attempt to rob them of their godhood. But is it? Certainly not. Your receiving does not take away from what they have.

It is not blasphemous for you to become one with them *in the way they have prepared for you*, for this is their desire. They ask you to become one with them.

- - - - - - - - - - - - - - - - - - -

Here is a caution. It is evil to want to do what Satan wanted to do, for he did want to rob God.

Remember that during our premortal existence, when Heavenly Father taught us his plan for our happiness and progression, Satan rebelled. He did not want to follow the plan. He did not want to follow Jesus. He did not want to receive from the Father. He wanted to change the plan to aggrandize himself. He wanted to take from the Father. He wanted God's glory. He wanted to become God.

He continues to oppose God and seeks to exalt himself.

> "Who opposeth and exalteth himself above all that is called God, or that is wor-shipped; so that he as God sitteth in the temple of God, shewing himself that he is God" (2 Thessalonians 2:4 KJV).

Because Satan rebelled against God during the premortal existence, he was cast out of heaven.

> "How art thou <u>fallen</u> <u>from</u> <u>heaven,</u> <u>O</u>
> <u>Lucifer</u>, son of the morning! how art thou
> cut down to the ground, which didst
> weaken the nations!
>
> For <u>thou</u> <u>hast</u> <u>said</u> <u>in</u> <u>thine</u> <u>heart</u>, I
> will ascend into heaven, <u>I</u> <u>will</u> <u>exalt</u> <u>my</u>
> <u>throne</u> <u>above</u> <u>the</u> <u>stars</u> <u>of</u> <u>God</u>: I will sit
> also upon the mount of the congregation,
> in the sides of the north:
>
> I will ascend above the heights of the
> clouds; I will be like the most High.
>
> <u>Yet</u> <u>thou</u> <u>shalt</u> <u>be</u> <u>brought</u> <u>down</u> to
> hell, to the sides of the pit" (Isaiah 14:12–
> 15 KJV).

Satan lied to himself about his own grandeur and power.

Because of Satan's rebellion, his opportunities changed. He was cast out of heaven and no longer has the opportunity to progress along the Father's plan to everything good as we do.

It is evil to want to replace God, to want God's glory. But it is not evil to follow God's plan and receive all things *as they are given to us* by the Father and the Son.

A scripture in Luke summarizes this important teaching:

> "<u>The</u> <u>disciple</u> <u>is</u> <u>not</u> <u>above</u> <u>his</u> [her]
> <u>master</u>: <u>but</u> <u>everyone</u> <u>that</u> <u>is</u> <u>perfect</u> <u>shall</u>
> <u>be</u> <u>as</u> <u>his</u> [her] <u>master</u>" (Luke 6:40 KJV).

We will never be above or more important than Heavenly Father, nor will we be above or more important than the Lord Jesus Christ. But the truth is we can become like them. We can become one with them. We can become perfect as our master is perfect. We can gain all knowledge. We can obtain all power. We can be all good.

The very reason Heavenly Father sent Jesus to the earth was to lead as many of his spirit children as would follow him back to the Father to become one in perfection with them.

> "For it became him, for whom are all things, and by whom are all things, in <u>bringing</u> <u>many</u> <u>sons</u> [daughters] <u>unto</u> <u>glory,</u> <u>to</u> <u>make</u> <u>the</u> <u>captain</u> <u>of</u> <u>their</u> <u>salva-</u><u>tion</u> <u>perfect</u> through sufferings.
> For both he that sanctifieth and they who are sanctified are all of one: <u>for</u> <u>which</u> <u>cause</u> <u>he</u> <u>is</u> <u>not</u> <u>ashamed</u> <u>to</u> <u>call</u> <u>them</u> <u>brethren</u> [siblings]" (Hebrews 2:10–11 KJV).

Note the teaching at the end of this scripture, the teaching that Jesus is not ashamed to call those who become sanctified brethren. If Jesus is not ashamed to call us brother or sister, we should not be ashamed to be his brother or sister. We should not be ashamed to become a joint heir with him. We should not be ashamed to become one with him. We should not be ashamed, despite our current weaknesses and imperfections, of our divine origin.

Do not let Satan deceive you into believing that if you deny the possibility of becoming perfect like God, you are being humble and honoring God. True humility, true Christ-like humility, is to accept what God teaches, to receive what he wants to give us.

Don't have a false humility that appears humble in the eyes of the world, that appears to honor God, but in reality, misunderstands, or accepts the philosophies of the world, or the deceptions of Satan. Everyone has the potential to become everything good just like God is everything good. That is Heavenly Father's plan. It is neither prideful nor blasphemous to believe that.

- - - - - - - - - - - - - - - - - - - -

Sometimes people struggle to understand if a scripture refers to Heavenly Father or Jesus Christ. Does "God" or "Lord" mean Heavenly Father, God the Father, or does it mean Jesus Christ, God the Son?

When you understand the "oneness" of God the Father and God the Son, how they work seamlessly and perfectly together to accomplish the Father's plan, you become less concerned if "God" refers to the Father or to the Son.

To understand scriptures, you don't have to dogmatically decide if a particular scripture refers to Heavenly Father or Jesus Christ. You can "get" the message by accepting the fact that whether it is Heavenly Father or Jesus Christ, the message is the same.

People who pray, people who talk about God, and people who write about spiritual concepts, often use terms like,

"God," "Lord," and "Divine," to refer sometimes to Heavenly Father and sometimes to Jesus Christ. This may perplex some people. However, using these terms interchangeably becomes common when a person understands the oneness between Heavenly Father and Jesus Christ.

ETERNAL LIFE

The promise of eternal life teaches our ultimate potential.

Jesus taught,

> "He [she] that believeth on the Son
> hath everlasting life: and he [she] that be-
> lieveth not the Son shall not see life; but
> the wrath of God abideth on him
> [her]" (John 3:36 KJV).

The apostle Paul taught,

> "That being justified by his grace, we
> should be made heirs according to the
> hope of eternal life" (Titus 3:7 KJV).

What is eternal life? What is this everlasting life that Jesus
wants us to have? Does it simply mean that those who follow Jesus will live forever, or does it have a deeper meaning?
It has a deeper meaning.

The scriptures teach that everyone, including the wicked, will be resurrected and thus "live" forever.

> "And have hope toward God, which they themselves also allow, that <u>there shall be a resurrection of the dead, both of the just and unjust</u>" (Acts 24:15 KJV).

All will be resurrected, the just and the unjust. This is a gift from Jesus Christ to everyone. Because he conquered death, all will be resurrected. Physical death is not the end of physical.According to Heavenly Father's plan and because of the Savior's resurrection, all will be resurrected, the spirit and the physical reuniting and remaining together forever.

However, those who strive to be good will be resurrected to a more glorious state than those who chose to be evil. The nature of our resurrection depends upon the choices we make.

> "Marvel not at this: for the hour is coming, in the which <u>all that are in the graves shall hear his voice</u>,
>   <u>And shall come forth; they that have done good, unto the resurrection of life; and they that have done evil, unto the resurrection of damnation</u>" (John 5:28-29 KJV).

God will resurrect everyone, those individuals that chose the good to the resurrection of life and those individuals that chose the evil to the resurrection of damnation, a stopping of their progression. The promise of eternal life is something special. Jesus taught,

> "And <u>this</u> <u>is</u> <u>life</u> <u>eternal</u>, <u>that</u> <u>they</u>
> <u>might</u> <u>know</u> <u>thee</u> <u>the</u> <u>only</u> <u>true</u> <u>God</u>, <u>and</u>
> <u>Jesus</u> <u>Christ</u>, whom thou hast sent" (John
> 17:3 KJV).

To gain eternal life means to know Heavenly Father and
Jesus Christ, not just know of them or know about them,
but to know them. Similar to how you know close family
members that you live with better than you know distant
unrelated people, having eternal life means knowing
Heavenly Father and Jesus Christ in a close familial relationship.

Remember that Heavenly Father and Jesus want us to become one with them. When we do this and thus truly know
them, we will be able to live with them and to live like them.
We will enjoy the happiness that they enjoy. This is what it
means to gain eternal life.

Listen to the message of the psalmist:

> "Thou wilt shew me the path of life:
> <u>in</u> <u>thy</u> <u>presence</u> <u>is</u> <u>fulness</u> <u>of</u> <u>joy</u>; <u>at</u> <u>thy</u>
> <u>right</u> <u>hand</u> <u>there</u> <u>are</u> <u>pleasures</u> <u>for</u> <u>ever-</u>
> <u>more</u>" (Psalm 16:11 KJV).

In the Father and Son's presence, we obtain a fullness of joy.
The Father's plan for our progression and happiness culmi-
nates back in his presence.

Jesus is the way. He mediates between us and the Father. At
an appropriate time, he will reveal the Father to those that
love and believe in him.

> "These things have I spoken unto you in proverbs: but the time cometh, when I shall no more speak unto you in proverbs, but I shall shew you plainly of the Father.
>
> At that day ye shall ask in my name: and I say not unto you, that I will pray the Father for you:
>
> For the Father himself loveth you, because ye have loved me, and have believed that I came out from God" (John 16:25–27 KJV).

Jesus can show us plainly of the Father. Jesus will fulfill his role as mediator between us and Heavenly Father, culminating with the righteous being with the Father. They will know the Father themselves. They will receive eternal life.

During our premortal existence, when Heavenly Father taught us his plan, he promised eternal life would be possible.

> "In hope of eternal life, which God, that cannot lie, promised before the world began" (Titus 1:2 KJV).

Heavenly Father's plan for our progression and happiness includes the "hope of eternal life", a promise of "eternal life" with Heavenly Father and Jesus Christ.

You can progress until you know God the Father and God the Son. You can live with them eternally, becoming like them, partaking of eternal life.

Heavenly Father wants to share Eternal Life with us.

Ears to Hear and Eyes to See

Symbolic teachings in the Bible teach our ultimate potential.

Jesus often used symbolism to teach important concepts. He encouraged people to have ears that hear and eyes that see. He wants us to understand. To those seeking to understand, symbols are powerful ways to learn about Heavenly Father's plan.

The symbolism within the Law of Moses, with its animal sacrifices pointing to the Savior's sacrifice, his atonement for sin, has been mentioned. Likewise, the symbolism of being born again, becoming the type of daughter or son that will be an heir of God and joint-heir with Christ, has been mentioned. The analogy of Jesus Christ becoming a Father to us and giving us all things as his Father gave all things to him has also been mentioned.

We will now consider four more prominent symbols that teach of our potential to become everything good: the symbolism of the Good Shepherd, the symbolism of the Tree of Life, the symbolism of the Bread and Water of Life, and the symbolism within the ordinance of the sacrament.

The Good Shepherd by Bernard Plockhorst

The Good Shepherd

Jesus said,

> "I am the good shepherd, and know my sheep, and am known of mine.
>
> As the Father knoweth me, even so know I the Father: and I lay down my life for the sheep.
>
> My sheep hear my voice, and I know them, and they follow me" (John 10:14–15, 27 KJV).

Jesus, the Good Shepherd, knows the Father; he also knows us, his sheep. He gave his life for us, both in how he lived and how he died. His sheep will hear his voice and follow him.

The time will come when those who follow Christ will be separated from those who do not.

> "And before him shall be gathered all nations: and he shall separate them one from another, as a shepherd divideth his sheep from the goats:
>
> And he shall set the sheep on his right hand, but the goats on the left.
>
> Then shall the King say unto them on his right hand, Come, ye blessed of my Father, inherit the kingdom prepared for you from the foundation of the world" (Matthew 25:32–34 KJV).

Those who follow Christ's way of living will inherit the kingdom prepared for them from the foundation of the world. Those who do not follow Christ's way of living will receive a less glorious state.

> "And <u>these</u> <u>shall</u> <u>go</u> <u>away</u> <u>into</u> <u>ever-</u><u>lasting</u> <u>punishment</u>: <u>but</u> <u>the</u> <u>righteous</u> <u>into</u> <u>life</u> <u>eternal</u>" (Matthew 25:46 KJV).

The "sheep" who follow the Good Shephed will live in the kingdom and know the Father and the Son, living like them, for this is life eternal.

The "goats" who did not follow the Good Shepherd will get everlasting punishment. Perhaps "punishment" means to not fully know the Father or the Son, to not live in their presence, to not live like them in their kingdom.

Remember, God is not mean. They will enjoy whatever degree of glory and happiness they are capable of receiving based upon the type of individual they chose to become. But similar to how a dam stops water's progression, those who deliberately choose to not follow the Good Shepherd stop their own progression.

The Tree of Life

The Book of Genesis tells of two trees in the Garden of Eden, the Tree of Life and the Tree of Knowledge of Good and Evil.

> "And out of the ground made the Lord
> God to grow every tree that is pleasant to
> the sight, and good for food; the <u>tree</u> <u>of</u> <u>life</u>
> also in the midst of the garden, and the
> <u>tree</u> <u>of</u> <u>knowledge</u> <u>of</u> <u>good</u> <u>and</u> <u>evil</u>" (Gene-
> sis 2:9 KJV).

The Tree of Knowledge of Good and Evil represents the fact that there exists both good and evil. Our Father in Heaven has given us agency that we may choose between them. The Tree of Life represents the state of those who choose the good and will partake of Eternal Life.

In the Garden of Eden, the Lord commanded Adam and Eve to not eat of the Tree of Knowledge of Good and Evil.

> "<u>But</u> <u>of</u> <u>the</u> <u>tree</u> <u>of</u> <u>the</u> <u>knowledge</u> <u>of</u>
> <u>good</u> <u>and</u> <u>evil</u>, <u>thou</u> <u>shalt</u> <u>not</u> <u>eat</u> <u>of</u> <u>it</u>: for
> in the day that thou eatest thereof thou
> shalt surely die" (Genesis 2:17 KJV).

Yet, Adam and Eve partook of the fruit. Did this then thwart God's plan? No. God's children cannot ruin his all-knowing, all-powerful designs. The events that occurred in the Garden of Eden were within the wisdom of him who knows all things.

However, because of the transgression, Adam and Eve's circumstances changed. They were expelled from the Garden of Eden and thereafter had to work for their sustenance. They became subject to death. Further, Adam and Eve could now learn the differences between good and evil and choose between them. They and the entire human family after them now have the ability and opportunity to distinguish and choose between good and evil.

In the Garden of Eden, Adam and Eve were somewhat naive, like little children. But now they could distinguish between good and evil. They could learn to choose the good and thus progress.

> "And the Lord God said, Behold, <u>the man</u> [woman] <u>is</u> <u>become</u> <u>as</u> <u>one</u> of <u>us,</u> <u>to know</u> <u>good</u> <u>and</u> <u>evil</u>: and <u>now,</u> <u>lest</u> <u>he</u> [they] put forth his [their] hand, and <u>take</u> <u>also</u> <u>of</u> <u>the</u> <u>tree</u> <u>of</u> <u>life</u>, and eat, and live for ever:
> Therefore the Lord <u>God</u> <u>sent</u> <u>him</u> [them] <u>forth</u> <u>from</u> <u>the</u> <u>garden</u> of <u>Eden</u>, to till the ground from whence he was [they were] taken" (Genesis 3:22–23 KJV).

Notice that the tree of life was forbidden. The message is this: lest by partaking Adam and Eve would live forever in transgression, not having chosen through experience either the good or the evil.

Consider the symbolism. Jesus taught that if we follow him, we will partake of eternal life. We will know God. The plan is for us to partake of the Tree of Life, but not until we learn to choose the good and forsake the evil.

The symbolism continues. The Tree of Life grows in the Father's kingdom.

> "And he showed me a pure river of water of life, clear as crystal, proceeding

out of the throne of God [Heavenly Father] and of the Lamb [Jesus Christ].

In the midst of the street of it, and on either side of the river, was the <u>tree of life, which bare twelve manner of fruits</u>, and yielded her fruit every month: and the leaves of the tree were <u>for the healing of the nations</u>.

And there shall be no more curse: but the throne of God and of the Lamb shall be in it; and his servants shall serve him

And they shall see his face; and his name shall be in their foreheads.

And there shall be no night there; and they need no candle, neither light of the sun; for the Lord God giveth them light: and they shall reign for ever and ever" (Revelation 22:1–5 KJV).

What a beautiful, wonderful place with the Tree of Life in the midst.

Hear what the following scripture teaches.

"He that hath an ear, let him <u>hear what the Spirit saith</u> unto the churches; <u>To him [her] that overcometh will</u> I <u>give to eat of the tree of life</u>, which is in the midst of the paradise of God" (Revelation 2:7 KJV).

The Savior will give of the Tree of Life to those that overcome evil. They will come into the Father's kingdom and be a joint heir with Christ. They will partake of the Tree of Life.

Not everyone will partake of the Tree of Life.

> "And, behold, I come quickly: and <u>my reward</u> <u>is</u> <u>with</u> <u>me,</u> <u>to</u> <u>give</u> <u>every</u> <u>man</u> [woman] <u>according</u> <u>as</u> <u>his</u> [her] <u>work</u> shall be.
> I am Alpha and Omega, the beginning and the end, the first and the last.
> <u>Blessed</u> <u>are</u> <u>they</u> <u>that</u> <u>do</u> <u>his</u> <u>commandments,</u> <u>that</u> <u>they</u> <u>may</u> <u>have</u> <u>right</u> <u>to</u> <u>the</u> <u>tree</u> <u>of</u> <u>life</u>, and may enter in through the gates into the city" (Revelation 22:12–14 KJV).

Let us obtain the right to the tree of life by obeying the commandments. Let us follow Christ's example. Let us choose good, overcome evil, partake of the tree of life, and live with Christ and Heavenly Father in their kingdom as joint heirs and truly know them, for this is Eternal Life.

Bread and Water of Life

Consider the following words Jesus taught when he was trying to lift people's understanding and expectations from worldly thoughts to holier thoughts.

> "And <u>Jesus</u> <u>said</u> unto them, <u>I</u> <u>am</u> <u>the</u> <u>bread</u> <u>of</u> <u>life:</u> <u>he</u> [she] <u>that</u> <u>cometh</u> <u>to</u> <u>me</u>

shall never hunger: and he [she] that be-
lieveth on me shall never thirst" (John
6:35 KJV).

At another time he had taught.

"But whosoever drinketh of the water
that I shall give him [her] shall never
thirst; but the water that I shall give him
[her] shall be in him [her] a well of water
springing up unto everlasting life" (John
4:14 KJV).

What is Jesus saying?

When someone understands the doctrine of becoming one
with Divinity, of what it means to gain eternal life, then that
person can see the symbolic meanings in Jesus's teachings. He
used the physical need for food and water to teach the spiritual truth that through him we can reach a state of complete
fulfillment, of not needing because of the wealth within.

The Sacrament

Consider the symbolic teachings found in the ordinance of
the sacrament. Before Jesus was crucified he instituted the
sacrament as a way for his disciples, including disciples of
today, to always remember him, to remember his example of
how to live, to remember his teachings, to remember his
great atoning sacrifice, and to remember covenants made to
keep his commandments and follow him.

"And as they did eat, <u>Jesus</u> <u>took</u> <u>bread, and blessed, and brake it, and gave unto them, and said, Take, eat: this is my body.</u>

And <u>he took the cup, and when he had given thanks, he gave it to them</u>: and they all drank of it.

And he said unto them, <u>This is the blood of the new testament, which was shed for many</u>" (Mark 14:22-24 KJV).

Jesus gave his life for us. He gave his life in how he lived, showing us the way to live. He gave his life for us in his death, sacrificing himself to atone for our sins. He gives us a resurrected life because of his resurrection. He gives us the opportunity of eternal life.

Jesus Christ accomplished what the Father asked him to do. Because of that, the Father's plan is fully operating for us. Because of Jesus Christ, we can and will become whatever type of individual we deep down inside want to become.

It is not the bread and the cup of the sacrament that saves us, redeems us, and sanctifies us. It is Jesus the Christ, the Beloved Son of God, the One chosen by God, the Great Jehovah, the promised Messiah, the babe in the manger; he is the one who saves, redeems, and sanctifies us.

The bread and cup of the sacrament help us remember him. He is our great hope. We should always remember him. We should worship him. We should follow him. We should strive to be like him. Because of him, we have the opportunity to become everything good.

- - - - - - - - - - - - - - - - - - - -

Symbolism is a valuable way to teach spiritual truths.

As you search for truth and study scriptures, as you ponder God's messages, use your understanding of Heavenly Father's overarching, all-encompassing plan to help you "see" and "hear" the teachings contained within the symbolism.

PRACTICAL

APPLICATION

TRUTH AND EVIDENCES

How can you know if the opportunity to become everything good is a true doctrine? After all, it is a very profound teaching that is not widely understood or accepted.

Plus, evil forces seek to deceive you. Deceptions and distractions come in many forms, dressed in pretty disguises to draw you away. Some people unintentionally spread falsehoods, with evil smirking as "good" people spread falsehoods. Others intentionally deceive for profit or status. Some people emphasize physical knowledge while discounting spiritual knowledge. Some mock spiritual teachings, claiming that spirituality and commandments are shams and that religions are for weak people or for controlling people. How can you avoid deception?

Plus, there is so much information in the world. Information abounds and bombards us. Multiple theories and ideas exist about—most anything. Statistics, "facts", positions, creeds, philosophies, assumptions, experiments, studies, reports, information, misinformation, all the stuff in the world can overload us.

The world's information continues to grow all the time. Scientific discoveries open new avenues for study. New theories and ideas arise with every generation. Old theories and ideas get discarded, with some arising again as "new" to another generation. Books, songs, movies, advertisements, sports, cultures, governing entities, religions, science, and multiple kinds of organizations plant and reinforce ideas in you every day. How can you learn the important truths?

Then there are those that will believe if they have proof. Well, no one wants to be deceived. We all like proof. With spiritual doctrines, however, the errant and easy-to-slip-into trap is that of requiring human-conceived methods for proof rather than using God's methods of learning. So, again, the question is how can you know?

With such a vast amount and variety of content on earth, how can a person learn valid truths? How can someone sift through the mountains of information and find the important truths? How can we learn spiritual truths in a physically apparent world? God will help us if we allow him.

Heavenly Father's plan includes the Holy Ghost whose very purpose is to guide us to the important truths, to teach us spiritual truths, to testify of Heavenly Father and Jesus Christ, and to give us peace.

God communicates with each person individually via the Holy Ghost, as they will accept it. This is why spiritual experiences, such as recognizing the communications of the Holy Ghost, are valuable. Each person can know for themselves the important truths regardless of what other people say, think, or believe.

We are spiritual-physical beings, with a spiritual body and a physical body. We are capable of learning in spiritual and physical ways. If someone limits themselves to only truths they can learn or prove physically, they are missing out. If we open ourselves to learning in spiritual ways, then God can teach us more effectively the important truths of how to become like him.

Spirit is not nothingness; it is, in fact, matter, a finer manifestation of matter than the coarse matter we call the physical, but it is matter. Spirit is just as real as physical.

Some people choose to reject spiritual experiences because they cannot connect them to physical experiences. That limits them. It's like throwing away the spoon and insisting on using a fork to eat your soup; it's much harder than need be.

Even though an overload of content exists for us to process in this world, human knowledge is still minute in the ocean of all knowledge, a few tide pools scattered about. When we learn—much, much—more than we currently know, we will see that all truths, physical and spiritual, mesh and work together.

Just because we can't yet fully understand how physical interacts with spiritual doesn't mean that spiritual is not real. Perhaps someday people will detect spiritual items using physical, human-based methods. But God has given us ways to know now. It is not wise to judge spiritual experiences as meaningless because they are not "proven" by physical methods.

Because God works individually and will not force anyone, confirmations of spiritual truths come in ways that are meaningful to the individual and not necessarily in ways other people will understand. This is a brilliant component of Heavenly Father's plan.

Many people want God to show tangible proof he exists. "After all," they reason, "if he is all-powerful, then why doesn't he show it?". People want concrete, scientific proof of God and spiritual experiences. They think God should perform within the realm of their reasoning, satisfying the conditions they specify.

But remember, humans don't know everything; God knows everything. He understands the big picture of eternity. His ways are better than our ways. He is helping us in ways that matter for eternity, whether we recognize those ways or not.

Spiritual experiences from God are just as real to the individual as the ground is physically touchable. Feelings are real. Thoughts are real. Peace within is real. Just because other people can't measure, don't feel, or can't recognize spiritual feelings at the same moment as someone else doesn't mean they are not real.

God communicates with individuals. His communications do not force or compel others to believe. This is brilliant.

Everyone chooses to believe or not to believe without being compelled.

Evidences of spiritual truths exist. People with open minds and looking for them can recognize the evidences.

> "Now <u>faith</u> <u>is</u> <u>the</u> <u>substance</u> of things hoped for, <u>the</u> <u>evidence</u> <u>of</u> <u>things</u> <u>not</u> <u>seen</u>" (Hebrews 11:1 KJV).

Substance and evidence of spiritual truths exist. As you accept these evidences, you become open to recognizing additional spiritual evidences; you see the influence of God in more and more situations.

In God's wisdom, it is those people that seek spiritual truths with an open mind and believing heart that find the spiritual evidences and receive the spiritual confirmations. Again, this is brilliant. It is also kind, with no one forced or compelled to believe.

God doesn't force. He shares and invites. It is important for us to choose the good while not having a complete understanding of everything because doing so reveals our deep desire to be good. Remember that in our premortal existence, we chose the "good" when we were "in-the-know". We were with Heavenly Father. We saw him, felt his love, and knew his goodness. We chose his plan, rejecting Lucifer's alterations.

Now is our opportunity to choose the good while not in Heavenly Father's presence, without physical proofs, but with evidences and personal spiritual experiences. This

causes us to grow spiritually because we are choosing to follow God based upon what we deeply want, and not because
physical evidence is so overwhelming that it compels us.

God's plan works for everyone on their spiritual level. Each
person progresses at their own rate and by their own
choices, desires, and efforts. Brilliant, brilliant, brilliant—
God is wise and kind.

At times in the history of humans, God sees fit for miraculous events or powerful manifestations to happen, such as
when Jesus lived his earthly life and performed many miracles. These powerful events can strengthen believer's testi-
monies, but they don't compel people to believe, at least not
for long, since the events aren't repeated and measurable as
if in a laboratory. Humans can find reasons to not believe
when that is what they want. God doesn't force people to
believe with miracles.

God decides when and where miraculous events happen.
Skeptics might think, "Of course, religious people say God
decides when and to whom miracles happen; it provides a
convenient haven to avoid the need for proof". But open-
minded individuals can see God's kindness, wisdom, and
love in allowing everyone to choose what they believe without compelling them with physical proofs.

Living by faith does not mean living blind to physical facts
or ignoring them; people who think this do not understand
faith.

A follower of Christ wants to learn all truth. She or he will
be open to physical and spiritual facts, to learning through

both avenues. But they will not abandon spiritual truths just because some of humanity's physical understandings don't seem to mesh with the "substance" and "evidence" of spiritual things.

As humans, we only know a small portion of all truth, a smattering of rocks and bushes scattered about in the landscape of truth. We should be humble and willing to learn more, instead of arrogant in our own knowledge. Some individuals will reject God's way of learning truth because they are so wrapped up in their own knowledge. Listen to how the following scripture describes them.

> "Ever learning, and never able to come to the knowledge of the truth" (2 Timothy 3:7 KJV).

It is possible for you to always be learning and still miss the important truths if you are unwilling to accept the manner God chooses to teach us these truths.

Be careful to not just follow the crowd. People receive emotional support by going along with the popular consensus. It is not surprising that in today's world, many people choose to trust physical "facts" and "proofs" over spiritual "evidences" and "substance", even over their own spiritual experiences, because science is so popular right now.

Humans have always wanted acceptance. This desire for acceptance can cloud our discernment of truth without us realizing it. In past societies, when religion was the widely accepted consensus, people received emotional support by going along with the then popular religious beliefs over budding scientific discoveries. It takes courage to search for and accept the important truths, whether they be physical or spiritual.

Many seem to believe that physical knowledge gives just cause to reject spiritual concepts. But their foundation is not as sturdy as they think. Gaps and contradictions exist in humanity's sum of knowledge. We simply don't see the entire landscape. "Facts" and "proofs" queue behind both sides of disagreements as people try to "prove" their understanding of the landscape.

Living by faith means not abandoning spiritual experiences you've had just because you can't "physically" explain them. It means to continue following God and striving to become more like him, even when you don't understand how some knowledge "fits" with other knowledge, or how to prove it to others, or even how to prove it physically to yourself.

Faith is believing in and trusting God because of the spiritual evidences you've discovered and because of your own spiritual experiences. Living by faith means exercising patience and wisdom, as you and the rest of the world learn more.

All truth does indeed mesh together, the physical and spiritual working together. Both are important in our progression to everything good. Someday we will see clearly how they work together.

Spiritual/religious people ought to be kind, open-minded, and willing to learn when other people present information that seems to contradict their beliefs. Non-spiritual/non-religious people ought to be kind, open-minded, and willing to learn when other people present information that appears to not align with their understanding of the physical world. You don't have to discard the things you know to listen to and learn from someone with a different point of view.

If you are striving to be like Christ, then you are striving to be humble, kind, open-minded, and willing to learn. We simply do not know it all, so we shouldn't act as we do. We should love, not fight, those that disagree with us or don't understand us.

- - - - - - - - - - - - - - - - - - -

Not all spiritual teachings, spiritual practices, or spiritual experiences are "truth" or good. Evil beings deceive using "spiritual" experiences just as readily as any other means of deception.

There are efforts to distort, twist, and change truth. Deceptions come in many forms.

> "Woe unto them that call evil good, and good evil; that put darkness for light, and light for darkness; that put bitter for sweet, and sweet for bitter" (Isaiah 5:20 KJV).

Things that enlighten or increase goodness come from God. Things that only appear enlightened or good on the surface, but underneath contain darkness and lead away from goodness, are not from God.

Evil imitations, spiritual charlatans, pious fakes, and the simply misguided will claim to be guided by the Holy Spirit, but God is not really with their teachings. In our search for truth, we need to be as Jesus counseled his disciples when he sent them out into the world.

> "Behold, I send you forth as sheep in the midst of wolves; be ye therefore wise as serpents, and harmless as doves" (Matthew 10:16 KJV).

Be wise in what you believe and harmless in your interactions with others.

Part of Heavenly Father's plan is that we grow spiritually by struggling against opposition. The multitude of philosophies in the world is part of the opposition that we must "struggle against" as we learn to discern truth.

We need to live by faith as we learn. It is good for us. However, as a person lives by faith and receives confirmations of truth, knowledge and experience begin to replace faith. The person grows spiritually, becoming more like Christ, with more knowledge and understanding concerning the things of God. A person can start believing in God by exercising a tiny seed of faith. Then. as knowledge and experience in the things of God increase, faith can grow into a strong, sturdy tree of knowledge.

- - - - - - - - - - - - - - - - - - - -

In our quest for truth, we should accept God's way of learning important truths, and not insist that he perform within our designated parameters before we will believe; otherwise, we probably won't gain the truth we seek.

Jesus offended some of his followers when he taught he was the "Bread of Life". He talked of followers needing to eat his flesh and drink his blood. Difficult teachings indeed. (See John 6.)

> "Many therefore of his disciples, when they heard this, said, This is a hard saying, who can hear it?
> When Jesus knew in himself that his disciples murmured at it, he said unto them, Doth this offend you?" (John 6:60-61 KJV).

It is easy to find fault with spiritual teachings when we judge them by physical standards.

Jesus let the people know his message was of spiritual concepts. He used symbolism, physical items to teach spiritual truths.

> "It is the spirit that quickeneth; the flesh profiteth nothing: the words that I speak unto you, they are spirit, and they are life" (John 6:63 KJV).

Physical means are not the way to learn of God, "the flesh profiteth nothing". We understand the things of God through the spiritual means God has established.

Those offended by Jesus's teachings left him.

> "From that time <u>many</u> <u>of</u> <u>his</u> <u>disciples</u>
> <u>went</u> <u>back,</u> <u>and</u> <u>walked</u> <u>no</u> <u>more</u> <u>with</u>
> <u>him</u>" (John 6:66 KJV).

Each of us will have occasions of "This is a hard say-ing". What will we do at those times? If we insist on us-ing physical means to understand the things of God, we simply will not get the message. We risk being offended by beautiful teachings or discounting impor-tant truths as meaningless. We risk rejecting the very things we are seeking—truth, purpose, and lasting joy.

Let us be wise and not reject spiritual truths. Our loving Heavenly Father has given us the way to learn the impor-tant truths. He wants to share with us everything good. If we accept his way and continue in his path, not insisting upon our methods, then the time will come when we will know and understand all things.

LIVING BY FAITH

For some people, the need to live by faith becomes a serious issue, perhaps a snag that trips them. Does God expect us to believe in him in the face of widely accepted physical "evidence" that, to many, seems to be against him, or to continue to trust him if life becomes cruel and unfair, or to continue trying to be like him when we are tired of the effort required and the other path looks so pleasing? Yes.

God expects us to live by faith, even when it is difficult. Exercising faith produces spiritual growth. Our time in mortality has a purpose. When it is difficult to live by faith, it is also an opportunity to progress spiritually.

Faith is an important part of mortality's learning experience. Yet, we can easily misunderstand faith. Believers and non-believers have misunderstood faith and that has led many away from God.

Some people mistakenly think that if we "have enough faith" we can cause what we want to happen; we can get

God to do what we want. But we do not control God. Faith is not a mechanism to swing worldly circumstances in our favor. Faith is more about trusting God while we learn to change our ways to align with his ways.

Blessings come from exercising faith in God, but God chooses the blessings. He is wiser than we are. Our mortal desires and urgency don't cloud his all-seeing wisdom. He decides how to bless those that have faith in him.

It is fairly easy for us to skip to wrong conclusions about faith when we contemplate Jesus's sayings "thy faith hath made thee whole" and "faith as of a grain of mustard seed" can move mountains (see Matthew 9:29 and 17:20). We might think that we are in control if we just have enough faith. But that's not quite right. God is in control, not us. Our faith becomes powerful and brings about miracles as it aligns with his will.

We all have much to learn about faith. Perhaps to exercise faith powerfully means to understand God's will, then in accordance with his will to exert ourselves spiritually, mentally, emotionally, and if needed physically to bring the desire about, deeply trusting God to do it, and to do it at the right time.

We need to strive to understand and accept God's will, and we need to develop our ability to exert ourselves in the right way, especially how to exert ourselves spiritually. Effort is the key. We learn these things by effort, by studying and pondering the things of God, by extracting meaningful lessons from life's experiences (even failures), and by repeatedly striving to be good, pure, and loving so we can have the Holy Ghost with us.

But performance is not the key. We can exercise powerful faith at whatever level of spirituality we currently have. A particle of faith exercised with deep trust in God can bring about miracles. Don't deny yourself the blessings of faith because you think you are not good enough. None of us are good enough. Kindly say to yourself, "I'll exercise faith because that is what God asks me to do."

If we can keep commandments when it appears futile to do so, such as loving our enemy even as our enemy hurts us, then that is a powerful manifestation of faith. Our actions of faith contribute to the blessing of all God's children.

Interestingly, many of God's purposes turn out to be the very things we desire and are praying for. But not all of our immediate desires fit within God's overarching purposes. As we learn to exercise faith, let us remember and not think of faith as a way to control Heavenly Father, or as a way to get what we want, but as an expression of our trust in him. Then, even when we don't get what we want, we will continue striving to live as God wants us to live.

When someone misunderstands faith, their belief and spirituality might be fragile. If results don't happen as they expect, then they can doubt their faith or doubt God's existence.

The previous chapter contained some of what it means to live by faith.

- Faith can start small as a person tries living according to God's way. (It can start from someone's good example, from the discoveries of spiritual substance and evidences, from small impressions from the Holy Ghost, or, perhaps, just from a desire to believe.)

• Faith can grow as a person continues living God's way and learns more about Heavenly Father's plan.

• Living by faith means not abandoning spiritual truths just because physical "facts" seem to contradict them.

• Living by faith means to continue following God even when others mock or scorn.

• Living by faith means having patience as we, and everyone else, continue to learn.

• Knowledge and experience can replace faith as a person understands more of the things of God.

Learning to live by faith is an important part of our progression toward everything good, and there is much to learn.

Humans are complex. If we can simplify the complex into simple components, perhaps we can see patterns and learn more about ourselves.

Let's reduce humans to just one desire—as a thinking exercise. Consider the following scenarios of a person, yourself perhaps. In each scenario, you have only one desire. Let's consider the beliefs and behaviors connected to that desire.

Scenario 1
Desire: your one desire is to fulfill your lust. (It doesn't matter what the lust is.)

Belief: believing in physical or spiritual items will not be important to you unless a particular belief helps you fulfill your lust. You probably put little importance on believing anything. Whether a particular belief is right or wrong is not relevant to you.

Behavior: you always choose actions most likely to give you what you want; therefore, you go after your lust regardless of what you believe or how your actions impact other people.

Scenario 2
Desire: your one desire is to be accepted (noticed, loved, appreciated, praised).

Belief: your beliefs likely flit around, matching the crowd you currently associate with, switching between believing in physical or spiritual items as needed. Whether a belief is right or wrong is not as important to you as the crowd accepting you.

Behavior: you always choose actions most likely to give you what you want; therefore, you do whatever the crowd does, so they are more likely to accept you.

Scenario 3
Desire: your one desire is to know truth (have knowledge, to understand).

Belief: you believe what you understand. You believe in physical and spiritual items as you come to understand them. Whether a belief proves to be right or wrong is very important to you.

Behavior: you always choose actions most likely to give you what you want; therefore, you search, seek, and study, always trying to understand.

Scenario 4
Desire: your one desire is to be better than others.

Belief: you might believe in spiritual items or in physical items, just as long as you appear to be right, more knowledgeable, or more capable than others.

Behavior: you always choose actions most likely to give you what you want; therefore, you act like you know it all and are probably somewhat snobbish. If you are religious, you condemn and look down on secular people who don't know what you know or don't think as you think. If you are secular, you condemn and look down on religious people who don't know what you know or don't think as you think.

Scenario 5
Desire: your one desire is to be good (loving, kind, selfless).

Belief: you believe what helps you to be good. It's easier for you to believe spiritual items simply because spiritual teachings encourage you to be good. You also believe in physical items when they enhance your ability to do good.

Behavior: you always choose actions most likely to give you what you want; therefore, you strive to be kind, unselfish, and willing to help others.

Humans are more complex than these scenarios. We all have some of each scenario in us, plus many more. But the scenarios illustrate the power of our desires. Everyone tends to behave in a manner most likely to obtain their desire, and everyone tends to believe in a manner most consistent with their desire. Desire drives what we do, and it drives what we believe. We can use this insight to help us understand our complex self.

Analyze your mix of behaviors and beliefs and you'll begin to understand your deepest desires. Be honest with yourself and search your soul. What you truly want tends to drive what you believe and how you behave.

Mortal life is important in Heavenly Father's overall plan. It reveals our deepest desires. With all the variety and options available during mortality, with all the good and evil, with all the evidences of physical and evidences of spiritual, with all we understand and all we don't understand, mortality is a crucible, with Heavenly Father's children learning what they truly desire.

Mortality is also an opportunity to mold self. If you don't like what you find through introspection, you can change. You can adjust your deepest desires.

If you want to become more like Heavenly Father and Jesus Christ, then you will come to accept the fact that we have to live by faith to develop characteristics similar to them. You will accept the fact that we need to struggle against intellectual opposition and exert ourselves in faith to understand the things of God.

- - - - - - - - - - - - - - - - - - - -

There are times during mortality when a person can take a giant step forward spiritually. But it may be difficult. When it seems God isn't answering our prayers, that we haven't had a spiritual experience for a while, or when doubts bombard us, perhaps, just perhaps, God is giving us an opportunity to advance spiritually in a major way.

Spiritually difficult times are opportunities to "live by faith" for longer periods or in a different manner than we are accustomed to.

We can use unanswered (from our point of view) prayers to develop more trust in God by choosing to continue praying, seeking, and learning about his will more than our own. We can use times of not actively feeling the Holy Spirit, of not having spiritual experiences, to show ourselves and God that, "I'm going to keep living by the commandments, because that is the type of person I truly want to be". And we can use doubts and conflicting "facts" to humble ourself, reminding ourselves that we have much to learn; so, "I'll keep learning, but not discard the spiritual truths I've already learned".

To get through spiritually difficult times, we can exercise our faith instead of abandoning it. We can use it like a tool;

then, similar to using a tool, we become better at our faith the more we use it.

Analyze your faith. Discover its foundation. If you find that your faith is built upon your culture or social circle and not upon your own spiritual discoveries and experiences, then it will be difficult for you to use faith as a tool in spiritually difficult times. But just as with every other part of our mortal experience, you can change that.

You can sure up your spiritual foundation, making it composed of your own spiritual discoveries and experiences, and not from what you are "supposed to believe" because of your culture. Then, during spiritually difficult times, it will be easier for you to exercise your faith as a tool; because your faith will be composed of who you are, not what other people think you should be.

Have you felt spiritual feelings? Don't dismiss them. Has the Holy Ghost prompted you in a certain direction? Follow it. Has the Holy Ghost taught you spiritual truths or confirmed truths to you? Accept them and don't cast them aside. Have you witnessed answers to prayers? Believe they came from God. Have noble thoughts enlightened your mind? Trust them. Have you seen God's goodness working in people's lives? Don't explain it away. Have you ever had faith in God? Keep it and use it.

Build your spiritual foundation a little at a time through your experiences and discoveries. Learn to notice the ways of God in your life and your foundation will become stronger.

Please don't dismantle your foundation of faith when life becomes more spiritually difficult than at other times. Cling to your own spiritual discoveries and experiences. They are yours. Heavenly Father works with you as an individual. Don't discard what he gives you just because you can't yet neatly place everything side by side in the compartments of your spiritually embryonic mind.

But also be sensible as you exercise faith. It is noble to think about using spiritually difficult times to increase our faith. But please remember that our spirit needs regular nourishment, just like our physical body needs regular nourishment. So, one of the best ways to get through spiritually difficult times is to seek spiritual nourishment.

Get spiritual nourishment by doing the basics of living in God's way, such as praying to Heavenly Father, studying and pondering scriptures, loving others, keeping the commandments, attending church, trusting God, serving others, relying on the Savior, etc. Our spirit needs us to do these things, whether we are experiencing difficult or easy times.

These basic tasks of spiritual nourishment help us traverse the deserts and the oases of mortality. They help us stay focused on becoming more like the Divine, and not get tossed about by "popular" or "current" philosophies that are the now thing.

In God's wisdom, he may give us valuable opportunities by delaying spiritual confirmations for longer periods than we want. Please don't interpret these times as God abandoning you, or that you are failing, or that God doesn't exist.

Interpret them for what they are, a chance to become more spiritually resilient by exercising your faith.

When Thomas, an apostle of the Lord who witnessed many of Jesus's miracles, doubted the Savior's resurrection because he hadn't physically seen him the first time the resurrected Lord appeared to the apostles, but believed after physically seeing him on the Lord's later appearance, the Lord used the occasion to instruct us all.

> "Jesus saith unto him, <u>Thomas, because thou hast seen me, thou hast believed</u>: <u>blessed are they that have not seen, and yet have believed</u>" (John 20:29 KJV).

We can have a believing heart and trust God even when we haven't "seen". After all, God is all-powerful. When we experience some of God's goodness, we can trust in him while we learn the rest.

> "Behold, <u>I am the Lord, the God of all flesh</u>: <u>is there any thing too hard for me</u>" (Jeremiah 32:27 KJV).

Let us be believing.

> "...<u>be not faithless, but believing</u>" (John 20:27 KJV).

REPENT AND OBEY
NOW IS OUR TIME

We are on the earth now. Our opportunity to experience mortality, learn from our experiences, and choose is now.

Each person acts and chooses for self. All of Heavenly Father's children, all over the world, whether they know of God's plan or not, have this opportunity.

Your thoughts, actions, choices, and efforts mold you. Where you live, your earthly status, your possessions, your wealth, the worldly thrills, the vanities, the fame, etc., these are only paint, decorations that are easily seen through when the person you built, the moral structure of who you are stands in the presence of Christ. You will be composed of what you truly love and the choices you made because of that love.

Jesus teaches us that he is the way to a life better than what we can create ourselves, a life better now and in the eternities.

> "He [she] that loveth his [her] life
> shall lose it; and he [she] that hateth his
> [her] life in this world shall keep it unto
> life eternal.
>   If any man [woman] serve me, let him
> [her] follow me; and where I am, there
> shall also my servant be: if any man
> [woman] serve me, him [her] will my Fa-
> ther honour" (John 12:25–26 KJV).

Life is more important than searching for pleasure. Life is about becoming. We should not be so pleased with our life that we are unwilling to change to become a better person. Heavenly Father loves all his children; but, as the previous scripture teaches, he honors those that follow and serve the Savior, our perfect exemplar.

Following are some basic principles and ordinances of Jesus's gospel as taught by him and his ancient apostles. The list includes the teaching followed by one or more scriptures. These basic principles and ordinances are valuable to know. They form the framework for following Christ.

- The good news is that Heavenly Father sent Jesus Christ to save and redeem us. Through him, we can obtain everything good.

> "For God so loved the world, that he
> gave his only begotten Son, that whoso-
> ever believeth in him should not perish,
> but have everlasting life" (John 3:16 KJV).

- Believe this, accept Jesus Christ. Have faith in Jesus Christ.

> "To him give <u>all</u> the <u>prophets</u> <u>witness</u>, that through his name <u>whosoever</u> <u>believeth</u> <u>in</u> <u>him</u> <u>shall</u> <u>receive</u> <u>remission</u> <u>of</u> <u>sins</u>" (Acts 10:43 KJV).

> "And Jesus answering saith unto them, <u>Have</u> <u>faith</u> <u>in</u> <u>God</u>" (Mark 11:22 KJV).

- Repent of your sins. Turn from evil.

> "Then Peter said unto them, <u>Repent,</u> <u>and</u> <u>be</u> <u>baptized</u> every one of you in the name of Jesus Christ <u>for</u> <u>the</u> <u>remission</u> <u>of</u> <u>sins,</u> <u>and</u> <u>ye</u> <u>shall</u> <u>receive</u> <u>the</u> <u>gift</u> <u>of</u> <u>the</u> <u>Holy</u> <u>Ghost</u>" (Acts 2:38 KJV).

- Be baptized when you have the opportunity by one who has God's authority.

> "And he said unto them, <u>Go</u> <u>ye</u> <u>into</u> <u>all</u> <u>the</u> <u>world,</u> <u>and</u> <u>preach</u> <u>the</u> <u>gospel</u> to every creature.
> He [she] <u>that</u> <u>believeth</u> <u>and</u> <u>is</u> <u>baptized</u> <u>shall</u> <u>be</u> <u>saved</u>..." (Mark 16:15–16 KJV).

- Receive the Holy Ghost and follow the promptings you receive from him.

"And we are his witnesses of these things; and so is also <u>the Holy Ghost, whom God hath given to them that obey him</u>" (Acts 5:32 KJV).

• Continue in Christ. Continue following the Savior. Continue repenting. Continue obeying. Continue learning. Remain faithful. Keep trying to be like Christ.

"<u>Not as though</u> I <u>had already attained, either were already perfect: but</u> I <u>follow after</u>, if that I may apprehend that for which also I am apprehended of Christ Jesus" (Philippians 3:12 KJV).

"Then said Jesus to those Jews which believed on him, <u>If ye continue in my word, then are ye my disciples indeed:</u>
And ye shall know the truth <u>and the truth shall make you free</u>" (John 8:31-32 KJV).

God will bless you with multiple and diverse blessings during mortality and in the life to come, as you build your life on these basic principles and ordinances of Christ's gospel.

"But he said, Yea rather, <u>blessed are they that hear the word of God, and keep it</u>" (Luke 11:28 KJV).

Any effort to follow Christ is worth the effort. Striving to live a Christ-like life is the right thing to do. The Savior's way of living, with the basics of his gospel and the keeping of his commandments, is the best way to live.

- - - - - - - - - - - - - - - - - - -

God gave us commandments that lead us along his path. His commandments show his love for us. God does everything in love. As we strive to be like him, we should receive and keep the commandments with love.

Jesus said,

> "If ye love me, keep my commandments" (John 14:15 KJV).

If you love the Savior, you will obey his commandments. If you love your pride, your passions, your possessions, or your sins, you will follow those paths.

Obeying commandments is really about love.

> "If ye keep my commandments, ye shall abide in my love; even as I have kept my Father's commandments, and abide in his love" (John 15:10 KJV).

Abide in Jesus and Heavenly Father's love, not just occasionally feel it—abide in their love. Joyfully, learn to keep the commandments.

What more could a loving Heavenly Father give you than this opportunity to choose to become like him. Choose the path to everything good.

Listen to the promises.

> "...they which are called <u>might</u> <u>re-</u>
> <u>ceive</u> <u>the</u> <u>promise</u> <u>of</u> <u>eternal</u> <u>inheri-</u>
> <u>tance</u>" (Hebrews 9:15 KJV).

> "And this is the promise that <u>he</u> <u>hath</u>
> <u>promised</u> <u>us,</u> <u>even</u> <u>eternal</u> <u>life</u>" (1 John
> 2:25 KJV).

> "<u>In</u> <u>my</u> <u>Father's</u> <u>house</u> <u>are</u> <u>many</u> <u>man-</u>
> <u>sions</u>: if it were not so, I would have told
> you. <u>I</u> <u>go</u> <u>to</u> <u>prepare</u> <u>a</u> <u>place</u> <u>for</u> <u>you</u>" (John
> 14:2 KJV).

Eternal life, eternal inheritance, a mansion in the Father's house, let us live so that we can receive the promises.

- - - - - - - - - - - - - - - - - - - -

It is an important part of Heavenly Father's plan that we strive to be good by keeping the commandments; but remember, we cannot save ourselves. We cannot bring these tremendous blessings to ourselves. Jesus bestows them.

So the question to consider is: upon whom will Jesus bestow the fullness of the promises?

As humans, we cannot judge each other's eternal outcome. We don't know how well someone is doing within the circumstances of their mortal life. We do not know who will inherit all that God has and who will not. Jesus taught us to not judge others but to strive to improve self.

"Judge not, that ye be not judged.

For with what judgment ye judge, ye shall be judged: and with what measure ye mete, it shall be measured to you again.

And why beholdest thou the mote that is in thy brother's eye, but considerest not the beam that is in thine own eye?

Or how wilt thou say to thy brother, Let me pull out the mote out of thine eye, and behold, a beam is in thine own eye?

Thou hypocrite, first cast out the beam out of thine own eye, and then shalt thou see clearly to cast out the mote out of thy brother's eye" (Matthew 7:1-5 KJV).

We are not to judge other people. We are to love other people. We are to improve self. Let us pull the "beams" out of our own eyes. Let us be kind in our thoughts towards others, for with whatever harshness we judge others that harshness is how we will someday look at ourself.

When we must judge, let us judge kindly and righteously, assuming the best. People are trying, just as we are trying. Have a helpful disposition instead of a condemning attitude.

Just because someone is baptized by God's authority and claims to follow Jesus Christ does not mean that person will automatically become everything good. Likewise, just because someone isn't baptized by God's authority and doesn't believe in Jesus Christ doesn't automatically mean that person will not become everything good.

Heavenly Father's plan includes everyone and all situations.

We simply do not have enough information to know upon whom Heavenly Father and Jesus will bestow all their blessings.

We can trust that Heavenly Father and Jesus will bless everyone to the degree that is right. They love everyone. They care for everyone. They are kind, merciful, and generous in their gifts.

Even though God will be generous to you, you must never minimize, not even a little, your need to obey God and live by the commandments. You should be honest with yourself about your efforts to be good and to keep the commandments.

Repeatedly, scriptures emphasize the need to repent and obey the commandments. Prophets of God, from ancient times to modern times, teach us to repent and obey the commandments. Apostles of the Lord Jesus Christ teach us to repent and obey the commandments. Our conscience and the promptings from the Holy Ghost teach us to obey God's commandments. Our parents, to the best of their ability, teach us to be good.

Most importantly, the Savior taught us to obey the commandments. He said,

> "Not every one that saith unto me, Lord, Lord, shall enter into the kingdom of heaven; but he that doeth the will of my Father which is in heaven" (Matthew 7:21 KJV).

He that "doeth" shall enter the kingdom of heaven. Words alone are not enough.

We must obey. This is not cruel. This is not restrictive. It is how we progress. The commandments are the way to travel the path that leads to everything good, to every desirable thing.

As we obey, let us not be arrogant and think that we "deserve" the Kingdom of Heaven, for without the Savior's grace and mercy, we will never enter therein.

> "For by grace are ye saved through faith; and not of yourselves: it is the gift of God:
> Not of works, lest any man [woman] should boast." (Ephesians 2:8–9 KJV).

We must obey, expending effort to be like the Savior, but the Savior cleanses our souls, not us. The Savior takes us to the Father and the promises, not us. We are the branches; he is the vine, without him, we do not bear fruit.

> "Abide in me, and I in you. As the branch cannot bear fruit of itself, except it abide in the vine; no more can ye, except ye abide in me" (John 15:4 KJV).

The Savior gives the increase. Without Jesus's mercy and grace, we would never bear the fruit of eternal life. But with Jesus's mercy and grace, our efforts to obey can bloom into fruit everlasting.

Don't let he-who-hates-you lull you into complacency and think you can enter the Kingdom of Heaven without humbling yourself enough to obey the commandments.

> "I the Lord search the heart, I try the reins, even to give every man [woman] according to his [her] ways, and according to the fruit of his [her] doings." (Jeremiah 17:10 KJV).

Learn from the experience of the man who came to Jesus wanting to know what to do to receive eternal life:

> "And, behold, one came and said unto him, Good Master, what good thing shall I do, that I may have eternal life?
>
> And he said unto him, Why callest thou me good? there is none good but one, that is, God: but if thou wilt enter into life, keep the commandments" (Matthew 19:16–17 KJV).

Jesus taught the man to keep the commandments to gain eternal life. The man asked which commandments he needed to obey.

> "He saith unto him, Which? Jesus said, Thou shalt do no murder, Thou shalt not commit adultery, Thou shalt not steal, Thou shalt not bear false witness,
>
> Honour thy father and thy mother: and, Thou shalt love thy neighbor as thyself.

> The <u>young</u> <u>man</u> <u>saith</u> unto him, <u>All</u>
> <u>these</u> <u>things</u> <u>have</u> <u>I</u> <u>kept</u> from my youth
> up: <u>what</u> <u>lack</u> <u>I</u> <u>yet</u>?" (Matthew 19:18–20
> KJV).

The man had been obedient. He had lived according to many commandments. He was in a position to learn more.

> "<u>Jesus</u> <u>said</u> unto him, <u>If</u> <u>thou</u> <u>wilt</u> <u>be</u>
> <u>perfect</u>, <u>go</u> <u>and</u> <u>sell</u> <u>that</u> <u>thou</u> <u>hast</u>, <u>and</u>
> <u>give</u> <u>to</u> <u>the</u> <u>poor</u>, and thou shalt have
> treasure in heaven: <u>and</u> <u>come</u> <u>and</u> <u>follow</u>
> <u>me</u>" (Matthew 19:21 KJV).

The message is clear. He had more to do. If you want to be perfect, there is more for you to do.

The message is: to gain eternal life "keep the commandments" and as you strive to keep the commandments, the Lord will lead you to perfection by revealing those areas of your life that you need to improve in, just as he did with the rich young man, "if thou wilt be perfect, go and sell that thou hast, and give to the poor" and "come and follow me".

We all need to "come and follow" the Savior. We all have parts of our life we need to "sell" and replace with holier actions. We all have patterns of life that the Savior asks us to improve.

To be a disciple of Christ means striving to improve, repenting as needed, obeying, trusting his grace more than our works, but always striving to obey.

Jesus obeyed his father.

> "<u>Though</u> <u>he</u> <u>were</u> <u>a</u> <u>Son</u>, <u>yet</u> <u>learned</u> <u>he</u> <u>obedience</u> by the things which he suffered;
> And <u>being</u> <u>made</u> <u>perfect,</u> <u>he</u> <u>became</u> <u>the</u> <u>author</u> <u>of</u> <u>eternal</u> <u>salvation</u> <u>unto</u> <u>all</u> <u>them</u> <u>that</u> <u>obey</u> <u>him</u>" (Hebrews 5:8–9 KJV).

Jesus obeyed the Father, and the Father blessed him with everything. If we obey Jesus, he will bless us with everything. This scripture does not say that Jesus is the author of eternal salvation to those that disobey him. It says he is the author of eternal salvation to those that obey him. Obedience is necessary; it produces spiritual growth and progression.

We do not have to live perfectly. Please don't pressure yourself. The Savior has power to save you no matter the depth of imperfection. Performance is not the key. Sincere effort, love, and not quitting are more important than excellent performance. Anyone can do these things.

If you are overwhelmed or don't know what to do to obey the commandments, consider doing something related to the first great commandment.

> "Jesus said unto him, <u>Thou</u> <u>shalt</u> <u>love</u> <u>the</u> <u>Lord</u> <u>thy</u> <u>God</u> <u>with</u> <u>all</u> <u>thy</u> <u>heart,</u> <u>and</u> <u>with</u> <u>all</u> <u>thy</u> <u>soul,</u> <u>and</u> <u>with</u> <u>all</u> <u>thy</u> <u>mind</u>.
> <u>This</u> <u>is</u> <u>the</u> <u>first</u> <u>and</u> <u>great</u> <u>commandment</u>" (Matthew 22:37–38 KJV).

Do something that shows God, and yourself perhaps, that you love him more than you love other things (or, at least, that you are exerting effort to love).

Or perhaps you could do something related to the second great commandment.

> "And <u>the</u> <u>second</u> <u>is</u> like unto it, <u>Thou</u> <u>shalt</u> <u>love</u> <u>thy</u> <u>neighbour</u> as thyself" (Matthew 22:39 KJV).

Do something that extends love to another person.

If you need to begin, start over, or simply continue on, do so by showing love to God and other people. Learn to love everyone in all circumstances.

Learn to love all people in all situations.

Jesus commanded us to love.

> "A new commandment I give unto you, That ye <u>love one another; as</u> I <u>have loved you</u>, that ye also love one another.
> <u>By this shall all</u> men [people] <u>know that ye are my disciples, if ye have love one to another</u>" (John 13:34–35 KJV).

A disciple of Jesus Christ strives to love others—there is no getting away from this reality. If you claim to follow Christ but do not extend love and kindness to other people, then you need to repent. A disciple of Christ loves—period.

One of the most important lessons to learn during mortality is to give love freely, without conditions. One of the most important characteristics to develop during mortal life is a loving nature.

Our love grows as our actions share love in a variety of circumstances. We need to learn to love in situations that are difficult for us to love. This is a powerful way to follow Christ; it has a powerful effect on ourselves and on others.

It may be difficult to always give love. Humans often seem to have an attitude of "us against them". We are comfortable with people that are like us and less comfortable with people that are not like us. Even in religions that teach us to love everyone, people sometimes are cold to or suspicious of those not in the same religion. Fear is easy. Love can be difficult.

Yet, there are people in almost every circle of life that are good at reaching out and including those not in the circle.

We should all exert effort to be like that. Love, kindness, and acceptance are some of the most important lessons we are on this earth to learn.

Diversity among humans gives us opportunities to reach beyond our comfortable boundaries and become better souls as we love those not like us. We need to soften our hearts and extend love to everyone in all circumstances.

We are not on earth to "fight the world". We do not need to prove "our way" as the "best way". We certainly don't need to control people.

We can share whatever good we have developed within ourselves, along with the truths we currently understand, and not demand that other people be like us. We can be Christ-like, with soft hearts, kind hands, forgiving attitudes, and loving actions.

The more we master the commandment to love, the more our capacity and desire to keep the other commandments expands. It becomes natural to obey the commandments. It becomes our nature.

Consider the amazing blessing promised in the following scripture to those that keep the commandments.

> "He [she] that hath my commandments, and keepeth them, he [she] it is that loveth me: and he [she] that loveth me shall be loved of my Father, and I will love him [her], and will manifest myself to him [her].

> Judas saith unto him, not Iscariot, Lord, <u>how</u> <u>is</u> <u>it</u> <u>that</u> <u>thou</u> <u>wilt</u> <u>manifest</u> <u>thyself</u> <u>unto</u> <u>us</u>, and not unto the world?
>
> Jesus answered and said unto him, If a man [woman] love me, he [she] will keep my words: and my Father will love him [her], and <u>we</u> <u>will</u> <u>come</u> <u>unto</u> <u>him</u> <u>[her]</u>, <u>and</u> <u>make</u> <u>our</u> <u>abode</u> <u>with</u> <u>him</u> <u>[her]</u>" (John 14:21–23 KJV).

This scripture, almost beyond mortal comprehension with its promise, declares that God the Father and Jesus Christ, the Lord of Heaven and Earth, will come and make their abode with those who keep the commandments. How can this be? It is fantastic. They do it because of their great love for us. We can learn to love as they love.

- - - - - - - - - - - - - - - - - - - -

Some people will accept Jesus and travel along the path for a time but not continue. They might become complacent, distracted, confused, or ashamed. Remember Jesus's parable of the sower with seeds. Some seeds began to grow but did not continue because of stony places and thorns.

> "But <u>he</u> <u>[she]</u> <u>that</u> <u>received</u> <u>the</u> <u>seed</u> <u>into</u> <u>stony</u> <u>places</u>, the same is he [she] that heareth the word, and anon with joy receiveth it;
>
> <u>Yet</u> <u>hath</u> <u>he</u> <u>[she]</u> <u>not</u> <u>root</u> <u>in</u> <u>himself</u> <u>[herself]</u>, <u>but</u> <u>dureth</u> <u>for</u> <u>a</u> <u>while</u>: for <u>when</u> <u>tribulation</u> <u>or</u> <u>persecution</u> <u>ariseth</u> because of the word, <u>by</u> <u>and</u> <u>by</u> <u>he</u> <u>[she]</u> <u>is</u> <u>offended</u>.

> He [she] also that received seed
> among the thorns is he [she] that
> heareth the word; and the care of this
> world, and the deceitfulness of riches,
> choke the word, and he [she] becometh
> unfruitful" (Matthew 13:20–22 KJV).

The cares of the world may cause some people to stop following Christ. Riches and desires for fame may choke the words of Christ. Persecution and mocking may cause one-time followers to take offense. Doubts or overbearing emphasis on physical knowledge may cause those who once believed to stop believing.

For some, it may seem too hard to live the Savior's way. Yet, he doesn't expect us to be perfect now. To the person you now are, the Savior's way may appear too long or too difficult, but your progression continues as you put forth effort, even if you don't notice the progression. So repent as often as you need to. Receive his forgiveness. He has already paid the price for your sins. He has shown you the way to live.

Become free by following Christ. Learn truths that expand your happiness, abilities, and opportunities. Give up the praises of the world for the peace that comes from loving and trusting God. Receive the peace Jesus gives.

> "Peace I leave with you, my peace I
> give unto you: not as the world giveth, give
> I unto you, Let not your heart be troubled,
> neither let it be afraid" (John 14:27 KJV).

Sincere effort to love and live as Christ loved and lived brings peace.

Striving to be Christ-like does not add pressure or judgments of flawless performance. At least God doesn't place those burdens upon us. We shouldn't place them upon ourselves. Pressures to "perform" are lies and attacks from evil forces, sometimes spread unintentionally by well-meaning individuals. Pressure can come from ourselves or it can come from others who either do not understand or who are trying to deceive or control us.

God's commandments are kind. Follow them the best you can in your current circumstance and trust God. As you do so, you can feel the Savior's peace. If you are sincerely trying, you are doing fantastic—you can trust the Savior's power to save you. He will not abandon you. Trust him more than your efforts at righteousness. But always strive to be good and to love like he is good and loves.

As you follow Christ, you will notice the areas of your life that you need to improve. This does not mean that you are bad or have failed. It simply means God is showing you a step you need to take in your progression. If you continue repenting, changing, and obeying, you will progress. If you continue on the path God shows you, then the time will come when, because of Christ, you will become like Heavenly Father and Jesus Christ good in every way.

Now is your opportunity to choose the type of person you want to be. The blessings exist. You can partake of them. Humble yourself enough to obey God's commandments and God will exalt you in due time.

"Humble yourselves therefore under the mighty hand of God, that he may exalt you in due time:

Casting all your care upon him; for he careth for you" (1 Peter 5:6-7 KJV).

"Blessed is the man [woman] that endureth temptation: for when he [she] is tried, he [she] shall receive the crown of life, which the Lord hath promised to them that love him" (James 1:12 KJV).

THE CHURCH OF
JESUS CHRIST—TODAY

Jesus described himself as "the way" to return to Heavenly Father.

> "Jesus saith unto him, I am the way, the truth, and the life: no man [woman] cometh unto the Father, but by me" (John 14:6 KJV).

To come unto the Father, we must do as Jesus prescribes, for Jesus is the way. We cannot rely upon human teachings or philosophies. We cannot follow false doctrines or false traditions, even religious traditions that are false no matter how pleasing to our sentiments. We cannot rely upon partial teachings of Jesus's way or upon twisted teachings of Jesus's way, realizing that there are conflicting ideas about Jesus and his teachings. We cannot rely upon human-made churches or human interpretations of the way. We want to live Jesus's way.

Jesus warned:

> "Enter ye in at the strait gate: for wide is the gate, and <u>broad is the way, that leadeth to destruction, and many there be which go in</u> thereat:
>
> Because strait is the gate, and <u>narrow is the way, which leadeth unto life, and few there be that find it</u>" (Matthew 7:13–14 KJV).

This is a profound teaching—relatively few will enter the strait gate and follow the narrow path that "leadeth unto life". It is available to all, but few will choose it.

Perhaps from our human point of view, it may seem that many people follow the path; but, from God's point of view, where he knows each of his spirit children individually, relatively few will follow the path that leads back to him. Still, it is available to everyone.

(Please don't assume that just because someone claims to be a Christian that they are living Jesus' way, or that someone who is of a religion other than Christian or no religion at all isn't living their life according to Jesus' way. Heavenly Father's plan encompasses everyone and we don't know enough to judge.)

If Satan and those spirits that followed him cannot totally lead individuals into evil, they seek to hinder them from completely following God. Perhaps trying to lull them into a false sense of security using partial truths, false ideas, or errant traditions and thus keep them from their full potential. "Strait is the gate and narrow is the way" that leads to life and "few there be that find it". But God is more powerful than Satan. He will help and guide anyone who truly desires truth.

Let's bring this to practical application. There are many religions and philosophies in the world. Portions of truth, portions of Heavenly Father's plan, can be found in many, perhaps all, of them. Within Christianity, there are many denominations. You can find truth to varying degrees within these church organizations. Further, to be a good and moral person you don't have to belong to a religion or church; you can just be good. Still, Jesus is the way. Partial truth isn't good enough for the person who wants to follow Jesus to everything good.

To fulfill our potential, we need to continue learning until we know all truths. This is accomplished through the way Jesus prescribes. We want Jesus's church to help us along the path. A church created by humans will not suffice. We want the Church of Jesus Christ. The church established and led by him.

During Jesus's earthly ministry, he called leaders to carry on the work after he returned to Heavenly Father. He gave them priesthood authority to perform ordinances. He told them to preach the gospel to everyone, to spread the good news of him, of the Father sending him to save, of his atonement for sin, and of repentance. He organized them into his church, with his authority, teaching his doctrine.

Today, with so many religions on earth and so many Christian churches teaching various doctrines, it would be a tremendous blessing to have the actual Church of Jesus Christ. Then we could receive a fullness of his way without gaps, false ideas, or misleading traditions.

The Church of Jesus Christ is upon the earth today. We do not have to do the best we can with remnants of truth revealed many years ago. His church is available today.

If the religion, church, or philosophy you currently adhere to motivates you to be a better person, that is fantastic. If it also encourages you to believe in Jesus and follow him, that is very fantastic. But whatever your current spiritual and religious status, please don't be so complacent that you bypass or don't recognize opportunities to learn more spiritual truths. God wants you to keep learning and progressing. Perhaps he will lead you to the Church of Jesus Christ during your mortal life.

How can a person recognize the Church of Jesus Christ and know that it is indeed the Savior's church with his authority, established by him, led by him, and not just another church that teaches about Jesus?

The Holy Ghost is the guide. As you learn spiritual truths line upon line and remain willing to learn, opportunities and truths open to you. To find the Church of Jesus Christ, you need to be open-minded and willing to receive more. You need to learn to recognize the feelings, thoughts, promptings, peace, and comforts that come from the Holy Spirit so that he can guide you.

How sad it would be for a person who loves Christ to reject his true church because he or she was too complacent in their current situation, or too steeped in a false tradition, or held fast to a false doctrine, or proved more concerned about social acceptance.

The Holy Bible can help you recognize the Church of Jesus Christ. But please be careful to not lead yourself astray. People interpret passages of scripture differently. Be careful to not convince yourself of something that isn't there.

The Holy Spirit guides.

> "Howbeit when he, the Spirit of truth, is come, he will guide you into all truth: for he shall not speak of himself; but whatsoever he shall hear, that shall he speak: and he will shew you things to come" (John 16:13 KJV).

More valuable than any "clue" we glean from the Bible will be the promptings and the guidance that comes from the Holy Ghost.

As you search for truth and the Church of Jesus Christ, consider the following elements recorded in the Holy Bible that were part of Christ's ancient church and that also relate to our potential to become everything good. See if the Holy Ghost testifies to you that these same elements exist within the Church of Jesus Christ today.

First, since it is true that we have the potential to learn all truth, to be cleansed from all sin, to progress spiritually and become everything good, to live with the Father as one, becoming joint heirs with Christ, then the true Church of

Jesus Christ will teach this. Because Jesus truly meant what he said when he said,

> "Be ye therefore <u>perfect, even as your</u>
> <u>Father</u> which is <u>in heaven is per-</u>
> <u>fect</u>" (Matthew 5:48 KJV).

The Church of Jesus Christ will teach that our ultimate potential is to become perfect, like our Heavenly Father. If a religion, church, or discipline does not teach this truth, then you may know that it only has partial truth. It may be a good church, a helpful church, but it doesn't have the fullness of the good news of Jesus Christ.

The Church of Jesus Christ understands the Savior's crucial role.

> "<u>Neither is there salvation in any</u>
> <u>other</u>: for there is none other name under heaven given among men, whereby we must be saved" (Acts 4:12 KJV).

The Church of Jesus Christ will teach that the only way to reach our full potential, being saved to the utmost, is through Jesus Christ.

Prophets and apostles are an element of the Savior's church. Anciently, Jesus called men to serve as leaders in his church. He is the head of the church, for it is his church, but he chose people to serve in various positions within his church to lead, teach, and help the members.

Today it is the same. Leaders in the Church of Jesus Christ will be called by Jesus's authority, not human authority, to serve within his church.

> "And he gave some, apostles; and some, prophets; and some, evangelists; and some, pastors and teachers;
>
> For the perfecting of the saints, for the work of the ministry, for the edifying of the body of Christ:
>
> Till we all come in the unity of the faith, and of the knowledge of the Son of God, unto a perfect man [woman], unto the measure of the stature of the fullness of Christ" (Ephesians 4:11–13 KJV).

The Church of Jesus Christ has apostles and prophets chosen by him to testify of him and his gospel as special witnesses. It has teachers that teach the gospel, pastors that watch over and care for the members, and evangelists that bless.

Of course, the Church of Jesus Christ will have prophets and apostles, for the Lord uses prophets and apostles to reveal his word to the masses.

> "Surely the Lord God will do nothing, but he revealeth his secret unto his servants the prophets" (Amos 3:7 KJV).

"Which in other ages was not made known unto the sons of men, as it is now revealed unto his holy apostles and prophets by the Spirit" (Ephesians 3:5 KJV).

This means that you can hear the word of God today through God's chosen servant, a prophet of God, in this age. This prophet will teach the same truths that prophets have always taught since the world began, but the teachings will be given in a manner that relates directly to today's situations and needs.

Jesus Christ remains the head of his Church, but he calls apostles and prophets to administer the church.

"And are built upon the foundation of the apostles and prophets, Jesus Christ himself being the chief corner stone" (Ephesians 2:20 KJV).

Jesus Christ
Head of the Church and Chief Conerstone

Apostles and Prophets
Foundation of the Church

These apostles and prophets serve within the Savior's church via revelation and inspiration from God; they can't just do whatever they want. It is Jesus's church.

The scripture quoted earlier (Ephesians 4:11-13) tells us why the Lord chooses apostles and prophets, why the Lord's church has this organization. These leadership positions are "for the perfecting of the saints, for the work of the ministry, for the edifying of the body of Christ". And these leaders are needed "Till we all come in the unity of the faith". This is a very visible element of Jesus's church.

Anciently, the church had 12 apostles, a quorum of twelve men. After Judas, one of the original twelve apostles, betrayed the Lord, Matthias was chosen to serve in his place, maintaining the quorum of twelve (Acts 1:24-26). This pattern exists today. The Church of Jesus Christ has a quorum of twelve apostles.

Another element of the Church of Jesus Christ is baptism. Jesus taught we must be born again.

> "Jesus answered, Verily, verily, I say unto thee, Except a man [woman] be born of water and of the Spirit, he [she] cannot enter into the kingdom of God" (John 3:5 KJV).

We must be born of water and of the spirit to enter the kingdom of God. Baptism is being born of water. Receiving and being sanctified by the Holy Ghost is to be born of the Spirit.

John the Baptist had authority from God to baptize. He taught people of Christ and called them to repentance. He baptized them as part of his special mission to prepare people for Jesus Christ. As directed by the Savior, John also baptized Jesus.

To enter into God's kingdom, we need to be baptized by one who has authority from God. Thus, within the Church of Jesus Christ, baptisms will be performed, and importantly, they will be performed by one who has authority from God, not authority created by humans.

This authority from God is another element of the Church of Jesus Christ. Anyone can organize a church and have it qualify by human laws as a church. However, if it is not done by Christ's authority, then it is not the Church of Jesus Christ.

Speaking of priesthood authority, Paul taught:

> "And no man taketh this honour unto himself, but he that is called of God, as was Aaron" (Hebrews 5:4 KJV).

People cannot honor themselves by claiming to take upon themselves God's priesthood authority. They must be called by God, under the direction of the Prophet and Apostles, just like Aaron was called to serve as a priesthood leader in his day, called by God via the prophet Moses.

In Old Testament times, when the Israelite people were not ready to receive the "Law of Christ", the Lord gave them the Law of Moses. Aaron and his sons were called by God to be priests and given authority to administer the sacrifices, rites, and priesthood ordinances of the Law of Moses.

The men of the Levite tribe were called to assist the priests. Only those Israelites who were called and set apart by God, the Levites, and the priests, had the priesthood authority to do these things. The other Israelites, not called by God to serve in the priesthood offices, not holding the priesthood, could not perform the ordinances and sacrifices. They could, of course, believe in God, obey his commandments, keep the Law of Moses, and receive the blessings of obedience. But only those called by God had priesthood authority to administer the ordinances and sacrifices.

This priesthood authority became named after Aaron and the Levites. It is called the Aaronic Priesthood, or sometimes called the Levitical Priesthood. This Aaronic priesthood is the authority John the Baptist had to baptize.

A priesthood ordinance, such as baptism, requires priesthood authority. John could not take this upon himself. He needed priesthood authority from God to have it be acceptable to God.

John the Baptist was a descendant of Aaron. Coming from the priestly lineage and as a called servant of God, he received the authority to baptize, along with a special mission to prepare the way for the Messiah.

Today, baptism, a priesthood ordinance, needs to be done using priesthood authority that comes from God, just as John the Baptist had priesthood authority to baptize. Within the Church of Jesus Christ, there will be those who have this authority, the priesthood authority of God called the Aaronic Priesthood, which authorizes them to baptize.

Now, just as the Law of Moses was a preparatory set of laws to prepare people to receive Jesus Christ and his higher law, the Aaronic/Levitical Priesthood is a preparatory priesthood, a priesthood that prepares for greater things.

The apostle Paul taught that perfection does not happen under the Aaronic/Levitical priesthood but requires further authority from God, a higher priesthood.

> "If therefore <u>perfection</u> <u>were</u> <u>by</u> <u>the</u> <u>Levitical</u> <u>priesthood</u>, (for under it the people received the law,) <u>what</u> <u>further</u> <u>need</u> <u>was</u> <u>there</u> <u>that</u> <u>another</u> <u>priest</u> <u>should</u> <u>rise</u> <u>after</u> <u>the</u> <u>order</u> <u>of</u> <u>Melchisedic</u> <u>[Melchizedek]</u>, and not be called after the order of Aaron?" (Hebrews 7:11 KJV).

Jesus Christ is the priest after the order of Melchizedek. We cannot obtain perfection under the Law of Moses, but under the gospel of Christ, we can. It is through the priesthood of Jesus Christ, the authority that Heavenly Father gave Jesus to be the Savior, that perfection becomes possible.

Paul referred to this priesthood as the "order of Melchisedic". Similar to how the preparatory priesthood became named after the man Aaron, "order of Aaron", so this higher priesthood authority became named after a man, "order of Melchizedek", the righteous King Melchizedek who had God's authority anciently. But it is not the priesthood of the man named Melchizedek; it is only named after him. It is the priesthood of the only be-gotten Son of God, the priesthood of Jesus Christ.

Whenever the Church of Jesus Christ exists on the earth, it will have this higher priesthood authority, the authority to perform ordinances continuing along God's path so people can reach their full potential. The Church of Jesus Christ will not only have the preparatory Aaronic Priesthood, but it will also have the Melchizedek Priesthood, the priesthood after the order of the Son of God.

Another element, and tremendous blessing, of the Church of Jesus Christ, is that husband and wife can continue to-gether forever as husband and wife. Families form the basic unit of happiness within Heavenly Father's plan. God de-sires men and women to marry.

> "But from the beginning of the cre-ation God made them male and female.
>
> For this cause shall a man leave his father and mother, and cleave to his wife;
>
> And they twain shall be one flesh: so then they are no more twain, but one flesh" (Mark 10:6–8 KJV).

Heavenly Father desires that husband and wife continue together.

> "What therefore God hath joined to-
> gether, let not man [woman] put asun-
> der" (Mark 10:9 KJV).

> "Nevertheless neither is the man
> without the woman, neither the woman
> without the man, in the Lord" (1 Corinthi-
> ans 11:11 KJV).

Men and women are equally important to Heavenly Father, neither "man without the woman" nor "woman without the man". A glorious blessing available within the Church of Jesus Christ is that husband and wife can become heirs together.

Listen to the message in the following scripture telling husbands to be good to their wife. Especially notice the promise of husband and wife being together forever (if, of course, they follow Christ and are good to each other).

> "Likewise, ye husbands, dwell with
> them according to knowledge, giving hon-
> our unto the wife, as unto the weaker ves-
> sel, and as being heirs together of the
> grace of life; that your prayers be not hin-
> dered" (1 Peter 3:7 KJV).

Husbands, honor and love your wife. She may become an heir of God alongside you and be with you for eternity. Wives, honor and love your husband. He may become an heir of God alongside you and be with you for eternity.

(Are you going to get stuck or offended by the phrase in the previous scripture "unto the weaker vessel", a phrase used long ago in a different culture, and miss the message God is trying to give us? Intuitively, we know women and men are equally important to God. So, let's not discount important teachings just because words or phrases don't align with current use.)

As a couple, individually important and choosing each other, husband and wife joined by God's authority may become heirs together in the Kingdom of God. Throughout eternity, they will continue as husband and wife.

God's power can seal husband and wife together forever.

The sealing power Jesus gives to the prophet and apostles of his church can bind families together forever.

> "And I will give unto thee the keys of
> the kingdom of heaven: and whatsoever
> thou shalt bind on earth shall be bound in
> heaven: and whatsoever thou shalt loose on

earth shall be loosed in heaven" (Matthew
16:19 KJV).

The Church of Jesus Christ has this sealing power, a power
that is a key of the Kingdom of Heaven, and this power will
be used to bind husbands and wives together so that they
may inherit together the eternal blessings that God has prepared for them. Families can be forever.

One more element of the Savior's church to mention now.
Think of all the people who have lived on the earth. Millions and millions of them never hear the gospel of Jesus
Christ. They can choose between good and evil. They may
be very good, moral people. But they do not have the opportunity to enjoy the blessings of Christ's gospel. What of
them?

Heavenly Father's plan encircles and provides for all the
earthly circumstances of all his children.

> "For <u>for</u> <u>this</u> <u>cause</u> <u>was</u> <u>the</u> <u>gospel</u>
> <u>preached</u> <u>also</u> <u>to</u> <u>them</u> <u>that</u> <u>are</u> <u>dead</u>, that
> they might be judged according to men in
> the flesh, but live according to God in the
> spirit" (1 Peter 4:6 KJV).

The gospel of Jesus Christ is being preached to "them that
are dead". Everyone, no matter when or where they lived on
the earth, will hear of Christ and his gospel and will either
accept Christ and follow him or reject him and his message.

Those who do not have the opportunity during their mortal life will have the opportunity after they die.

Heavenly Father's plan includes the time before we came to earth and it includes the time after we die. God loves all his children. Each of Heavenly Father's children can progress toward perfection by accepting Christ and living by the principles of his gospel.

Thus, the Church of Jesus Christ will teach that everyone, regardless of individual earthly circumstances, will have a fair opportunity to hear and accept Christ's gospel.

Thoughtful readers may wonder how individuals that didn't have the opportunity during their mortal life to hear the gospel can be baptized. After all, one must be baptized by the proper authority to enter the Kingdom of God.

God provides for all contingencies. All who accept Jesus Christ and his gospel will receive the blessings of baptism, even those who did not have the opportunity during their mortal life.

> "Else what shall they do <u>which are baptized for the dead</u>, if the dead rise not at all? why are they then baptized for the dead" (1 Corinthians 15:29 KJV).

Members of the Church of Jesus Christ will understand proxy baptism for those who have died. Members of the Church of Jesus Christ perform these proxy baptisms by the priesthood authority of Jesus Christ, the Melchizedek priesthood.

In summary, the Church of Jesus Christ will contain at least these elements that relate to our potential to progress to everything good.

- First, it will teach that perfection is possible, the exalting climax of Heavenly Father's plan for our happiness.

- Second, it will teach that because of Jesus Christ and only through Jesus Christ can one reach their full potential.

- Third, it will be organized with a prophet and apostles, along with other positions to administer, teach, and help its members in the Savior's path.

- Fourth, its members will be baptized, a requirement for entrance into the Kingdom of Heaven.

- Fifth, it will have the Aaronic priesthood to perform baptisms using God's authority.

- Sixth, it will have the higher priesthood, the Melchizedek priesthood, the authority to perform higher ordinances.

- Seventh, it will have the sealing power to bind husbands and wives together (one of the higher ordinances) so that they may become heirs together.

• Eighth, it will teach that everyone, regardless of when or where they lived on earth, will have the opportunity to hear of Christ and his gospel and either accept him, receive the blessings of membership in his church, or to reject him. Accordingly, members of the Church of Jesus Christ will understand proxy ordinances and do baptisms for those who have died without the opportunity.

Let us be vigilant in searching for and receiving truth. As you sincerely desire truth, perhaps the Holy Ghost will lead you to the Church of Jesus Christ, and then you can partake of the blessings of membership in Christ's church during your mortal life.

TESTIMONY

Heavenly Father respects us as individuals and works individually with each of us. Everyone can receive inspiration, revelation, and confirmations of truths directly from him via the Holy Ghost, just like Peter, one of Christ's ancient apostles did. In the following scripture, Peter is called Simon Bar-jona.

> "And Jesus answered and said unto him, <u>Blessed</u> <u>art</u> <u>thou</u>, <u>Simon</u> <u>Bar-jona</u>: <u>for</u> <u>flesh</u> <u>and</u> <u>blood</u> <u>hath</u> <u>not</u> <u>revealed</u> <u>it</u> <u>unto</u> <u>thee</u>, <u>but</u> <u>my</u> <u>Father</u> <u>which</u> <u>is</u> <u>in</u> <u>heaven</u>" (Matthew 16:17 KJV).

"Flesh and blood" didn't reveal spiritual truths to Peter, but Heavenly Father did. We can gain our witness of truth as Heavenly Father sends us understanding and confirmations via the Holy Ghost.

We can share our testimony of the things God has taught us. But if people don't understand or choose to not accept our testimony, that is okay. We can be kind and not force, demand, or judge. God doesn't compel; neither should we.

God loves everyone without conditions. If we are truly striving to become everything good, then we must also learn to love without conditions and let people progress spiritually as they choose and are ready.

We shouldn't try to force anyone to learn the things of God. We should share what we have so they have opportunities to learn if they so choose.

> "<u>As every man</u> [woman] <u>hath received the gift, even so minister the same one to another</u>, as good stewards of the manifold grace of God" (1 Peter 4:10 KJV).

In this world where much evil exists, with people searching for lasting happiness and wanting meaningful existence, one of the best things we can do is to be an example of Christlike living, striving to live and love as Christ lived and loved.

> "<u>Let your light so shine before men</u> [all]<u>, that they may see your good works, and glorify your Father which is in heaven</u>" (Matthew 5:16 KJV).

Don't force and condemn. Love and share. Be a light, not for praise or show, but from love. This is Heavenly Father's way of spreading the message of his plan. This is Heavenly Father's way of spreading the good news of the Savior. Preach and teach when it is appropriate. But always love and "shine" by striving to be like Christ.

While we shouldn't try to force anyone to learn the things of God, we also don't need to wait for anyone. Each person progresses spiritually as fast and as far as they choose, by how willing they are to follow God's guidance via the Holy Ghost. We each can gain our own testimony of spiritual truths, independent of any other person.

- - - - - - - - - - - - - - - - - - -

A Testimony from the Author

I testify God exists. He is kind and loving. He is the father of our spirits, our Heavenly Father. I know he cares for each of us. I testify that he loves you unconditionally. If you can accept that fact, you can feel his love. I invite you to pray to Heavenly Father and share your heart with him. Feel his love and receive the messages he sends to you.

I testify that Jesus Christ is the Son of God, the only begotten son of the Father in the flesh. He is the Savior. His example is the way to live. Lasting happiness comes from striving to be like him. I invite you to believe Jesus Christ and follow him.

I testify that everyone, whether during this mortal life or after death, will hear the gospel of Jesus Christ and will either accept it or reject it. I invite you to accept Christ and become a baptized member of the Church of Jesus Christ when you have that opportunity.

I testify that Heavenly Father's plan for our happiness and progression is beautiful and complete. I testify that because of God's love, we have agency and opportunities. We can choose to become whatever type of person we deeply want to become. I invite you to thank Heavenly Father for this opportunity.

I invite you to repent as needed. I testify that because of Jesus Christ, we can change from bad to good, from good to very good, and from very good to everything good. I invite you to follow Jesus Christ and continue to follow him. I testify he is the way to all that is good.

I know these things because of the peace and spiritual confirmations I've felt from the Holy Ghost. I share this testimony with you in the sacred name of Jesus Christ. Amen.

CLOSING THOUGHTS

The psalmist beautifully declared,

> "For the Lord God is a sun and shield:
> the Lord will give grace and glory: no good
> thing will he withhold from them that
> walk uprightly" (Psalm 84:11 KJV).

The Lord gives grace and glory. No good thing will he withhold from you if you "walk uprightly".

Truths are eternal. The truths taught by the Lord's servants today are the same truths taught anciently by the Lord's servants. The need to love people, repent of sins, and keep God's commandments apply to everyone, everywhere, at any time in the earth's history. The way to follow Jesus Christ doesn't change.

> "Jesus Christ the same yesterday,
> and to day, and for ever" (Hebrews 13:8
> KJV).

If you are searching and not finding, confused about life, or don't understand, perhaps you have not been taught applicable truths of Heavenly Father's plan, or maybe you have chosen to not receive them. Perhaps you are following the philosophies of the world.

Many of Heavenly Father's children are not willing to learn more truths and keep progressing spiritually towards everything good, simply because they are content with the truths they already know, or because they want worldly praise more than spiritual growth, or perhaps they cling to a false tradition or hold fast to a false doctrine.

Consider this: as someone goes through mortal life, that person learns a marvelous truth. Perhaps he or she learns that Jesus Christ is the Savior, and accepts this truth, loving the Savior.

But, suppose that person then allows the adversary to lull him or her into complacency, stopping their progression, or they later decide to reject what they once believed, again stopping their progression. Or suppose that person allows false teachings about Jesus to lead them off the strait and narrow path, thinking all the time that they are okay because of that first great truth they learned. Or suppose that person strays from their original commitment and follows their lusts into sin. We all need to be vigilant to not stop our spiritual progression.

Whatever mortal life is like for you, whatever your understanding of Heavenly Father's plan, you need to be humble and admit to yourself that you do not know all things, even if you know many things or know some things in great detail.

We all need to be humble and willing to be taught, willing to receive truths when we have opportunities. We need to continue to learn line upon line.

If you are searching or unhappy, perhaps you are living by human philosophies instead of by Heavenly Father's Plan of Happiness.

If you are sincere in wanting to be good, promptings from the Holy Ghost will guide you. As you follow those promptings, you will continue to receive guidance as God sees fit. You will progress and learn line upon line. Perhaps during your mortal life, God will lead you to the Church of Jesus Christ, where you can learn a fullness of the good news.

Remember that as you exercise faith and strive to follow Jesus, God doesn't pressure or burden you with the need to be perfect. If you feel pressure to be perfect, perhaps you are thinking too highly of your own abilities, or perhaps you are seeking approval or praise, or maybe you simply don't understand yet.

Take pressure off yourself by trusting God. Simply love and serve others, remain willing to learn and change, obey the commandments, strive to be like Jesus, and repent as needed (do these things without thinking you have to do them perfectly). Good things will happen. You will become a better individual, a more Christ-like individual, and the Holy Ghost will lead you.

God is giving us an opportunity to "buy" a pearl of great price, by giving all our heart, might, mind, and strength to him—to love him fully and live his way.

> "Again, the kingdom of heaven is like unto a merchant man, seeking goodly pearls:
> Who, when he had found one pearl of great price, went and sold all that he had, and bought it" (Matthew 13:45–46 KJV).

Every effort to follow Jesus Christ and obtain the kingdom of heaven is worth the effort.

I'll end this book by echoing the following admonition from the apostle Paul.

> "Therefore leaving the principles of the doctrine of Christ, <u>let us go on unto perfection</u>; not laying again the foundation of repentance from dead works, and of faith toward God" (Hebrews 6:1 KJV).

Let us go on unto perfection. As a spirit child of Heavenly Father, take the truth that you currently have and don't lay the foundation again and again staying on the same spiritual plateau; move onward, reaching higher plateaus.

Follow Christ to the best of your abilities. Be humble, and willing to receive more from God. Repent of your sins, and let Jesus Christ cleanse you. Gain more knowledge. Lay aside false notions and traditions. Be wise in what you believe. Obey the commandments. Love God. Love other people; learn to love in all circumstances.

When you have the opportunity, be baptized into the Church of Jesus Christ. Remain faithful and diligent. Continue following Christ. Trust him to amply supply, compensating for your inadequacies, healing your hurts, changing your imperfections. Receive all that Heavenly Father and the Lord Jesus Christ through their mercy, grace, and love have prepared for you.

Go on unto perfection. Do not stop. Do not give in to evil. Keep striving to be good. Keep striving to love as God loves. No matter what setbacks befall you, no matter how many times you fall short and sin, continue on. Repent and continue following Christ.

Because of Jesus Christ, you can make it. His way creates lasting happiness. His way brings fullness of joy. Through him, you will have great peace. With him, you will become everything good.

Go on unto perfection.

"...trees of righteousness, the planting
of the Lord..." (Isaiah 61:3 KJV).

ADDITIONAL

ITEMS

APPENDIX 1
A SECOND WITNESS OF CHRIST

The Holy Bible is a very valuable witness of Jesus Christ. God lovingly gives us more than just the Bible to learn about Jesus and the plan for our happiness.

The Book of Mormon, Another Testament of Jesus Christ, is a book of scripture comparable to the Holy Bible, given by God for our benefit. It teaches the same truths as the Bible.

When a seeker of truth studies both sets of scriptures, clarity emerges from the complementary teachings and witnesses.

The Holy Bible is a record of God's dealings with a group of ancient people in the "old world". The Book of Mormon is a record of God's dealings with a group of ancient people in the Americas. Both books testify that Jesus Christ is the Son of God, the Savior and Redeemer of the world, the

Way to live. Both books contain the gospel of Jesus Christ.

One purpose of the author's book is to show that the Holy
Bible teaches our ultimate potential. Accordingly, I used
scriptures from the Holy Bible only in the main content. In
this appendix, I share one scripture from the Book of Mormon that parallel teaches and second witnesses many of the
points presented in this book.

> "Yea, <u>come</u> <u>unto</u> <u>Christ</u>, <u>and</u> <u>be</u> <u>per-</u>
> <u>fected</u> <u>in</u> <u>him</u>, and deny yourselves of all
> ungodliness, and if ye shall deny your-
> selves of all ungodliness, and <u>love</u> <u>God</u>
> <u>with</u> <u>all</u> <u>your</u> <u>might,</u> <u>mind</u> <u>and</u> <u>strength,</u>
> then is <u>his</u> <u>grace</u> <u>sufficient</u> <u>for</u> <u>you,</u> that <u>by</u>
> <u>his</u> <u>grace</u> <u>ye</u> <u>may</u> <u>be</u> <u>perfect</u> <u>in</u> <u>Christ;</u> and
> if by the grace of God ye are perfect in
> Christ, ye can in nowise deny the power of
> God.
> And again, if ye by the grace of God
> are perfect in Christ, and deny not his
> power, <u>then</u> <u>are</u> <u>ye</u> <u>sanctified</u> <u>in</u> <u>Christ</u> <u>by</u>
> <u>the</u> <u>grace</u> <u>of</u> <u>God,</u> <u>through</u> <u>the</u> <u>shedding</u> <u>of</u>
> <u>the</u> <u>blood</u> <u>of</u> <u>Christ</u>, which is in the
> covenant of the Father unto the remission
> of your sins, that <u>ye</u> <u>become</u> <u>holy,</u> <u>without</u>
> <u>spot</u>" (Moroni 10:32–33 Book of Mormon).

Two witnesses work together and provide clarity.

If you want to study the Book of Mormon, you can find it
online at: churchofjesuschrist.org/study/scriptures/bofm.

APPENDIX 2
RELIGIOUS AFFILIATION

The author's religion isn't mentioned in the book's main text. It isn't needed. But since this book is about spiritual topics, some readers may be interested in the author's religion.

The solution became to include it in an appendix for anyone that may be wondering. So, here it is.

I am a member of The Church of Jesus Christ of Latter-day Saints, a worldwide religion open to anyone. I participate fully in the local congregation where I live.

If you want more information about The Church of Jesus Christ of Latter-day Saints, you can visit the Church's website at churchofjesuschrist.org.

Scripture Index

Listed in order of *To Everything Good*

A Beautiful Teaching
2 Timothy 3:16–17 6
Isaiah 42:16 8
Isaiah 61:3 8
John 14:26 9

The Plan of Progression and Happiness
Revelation 12:7–9 13
Isaiah 55:8–9 22
Psalm 89:14 23
Psalm 19:9 23
Revelation 15:3 23

Follow Jesus
Luke 9:23 27
Matthew 10:38 28

Matthew 7:24 28
Matthew 5:48 30
John 14:6 31
John 15:4–5 32

Salvation
Matthew 1:21 35
Romans 3:23 36
Hebrews 7:25 37
Isaiah 1:18 38
Titus 2:14 38
Hebrews 10:1 39
Hebrews 10:10,14–15 39

Heirs and Joint–heirs
Hebrews 12:9 41
Genesis 1:27 42

Acts 17:28–29   42
Romans 8:16   43
Romans 8:17   43
John 1:12   44
John 3:3   44
John 3:5   45
Galatians 4:7   45
Revelation 3:21–22   46

**The Father, The Son, and
Us**
John 3:16   49
John 5:19   50
John 8:29   50
John 8:28   50
John 3:35   50
2 Corinthians 6:17–18   51
Revelation 21:7   51
Matthew 7:7–8   52
Mark 4: 23–24   53
Isaiah 28:9–10   54
2 Peter 1:3   54
John 16:13   55

Become One
John 10:30   57
John 10:34–36   58
John 10:37–38   59
Philippians 2:5–6   59
John 17:20–23   60
2 Thessalonians 2:4   62
Isaiah 14:12–15   63

Luke 6:40   63
Hebrews 2:10–11   64

Eternal Life
John 3:36   67
Titus 3:7   67
Acts 24:15   68
John 5:28–29   68
John 17:3   69
Psalm 16:11   69
John 16:25–27   70
Titus 1:2   70

**Ears to Hear and Eyes to
See**
John 10:14–15, 27   75
Matthew 25:32–34   75
Matthew 25:46   76
Genesis 2:9   77
Genesis 2:17   77
Genesis 3:22–23   78
Revelation 22:1–5   78-9
Revelation 2:7   79
Revelation 22:12–14   80
John 6:35   80-1
John 4:14   81
Mark 14:22-24   82

Truth and Evidences
Hebrews 11:1   91
2 Timothy 3:7   93
Isaiah 5: 20   95

Matthew 10:16	96	Matthew 19:16–17	120
John 6:60-61	97	Matthew 19:18–20	120-1
John 6:63	97	Matthew 19:21	121
John 6:66	98	Hebrews 5:8–9	122
		Matthew 22:37–38	122
Living by Faith		Matthew 22:39	123
John 20:29	109	John 13:34–35	124
Jeremiah 32:27	109	John 14:21–23	125-6
John 20:27	109	Matthew 13:20–22	126-7
		John 14:27	127
Repent and Obey, Now is Our Time		1 Peter 5:6–7	129
		James 1:12	129
John 12:25–26	112		
John 3:16	112	**The Church of Jesus Christ —Today**	
Acts 10:43	113		
Mark 11:22	113	John 14:6	131
Acts 2:38	113	Matthew 7:13–14	132
Mark 16:15–16	113	John 16:13	135
Acts 5:32	114	Matthew 5:48	136
Philippians 3:12	114	Acts 4:12	136
John 8:31–32	114	Ephesians 4:11–13	137
Luke 11:28	114	Amos 3:7	137
John 14:15	115	Ephesians 3:5	138
John 15:10	115	Ephesians 2:20	138
Hebrews 9:15	116	John 3:5	139
1 John 2:25	116	Hebrews 5:4	140
John 14:2	116	Hebrews 7:11	142
Matthew 7:1–5	117	Mark 10:6–8	143
Matthew 7:21	118	Mark 10:9	144
Ephesians 2:8–9	119	1 Corinthians 11:11	144
John 15:4	119	1 Peter 3:7	144
Jeremiah 17:10	120	Matthew 16:19	145-6

1 Peter 4:6   146   **Closing Thoughts**
1 Corinthians 15:29   147   Psalm 84:11   155
                                   Hebrews 13:8   155
Testimony   Matthew 13:45–46   158
Matthew 16:17   151   Hebrews 6:1   159
1 Peter 4:10   152   Isaiah 61:3   161
Matthew 5:16   152

Listed in order of the *Holy Bible*

Old Testament   Isaiah 28:9–10   54
                                   Isaiah 42:16   8
Genesis   Isaiah 55:8–9   22
Genesis 1:27   42   Isaiah 61:3   8 and 161
Genesis 2:9   77
Genesis 2:17   77   **Jeremiah**
Genesis 3:22–23   78   Jeremiah 17:10   120
                                   Jeremiah 32:27   109
Psalms
Psalm 16:11   69   **Amos**
Psalm 19:9   23   Amos 3:7   137
Psalm 84:11   155
Psalm 89:14   23
                                   New Testament
Isaiah
Isaiah 1:18   38   **Matthew**
Isaiah 5:20   95   Matthew 1:21   35
Isaiah 14:12–15   63   Matthew 5:16   152

Matthew 5:48 30 and 136

Matthew 7:1–5   117

Matthew 7:7–8   52

Matthew 7:13–14   132

Matthew 7:21   118

Matthew 7:24   28

Matthew 10:16   96

Matthew 10:38   28

Matthew 13:20–22 126-7

Matthew 13:45–46   158

Matthew 16:17   151

Matthew 16:19   145-6

Matthew 19:16–17   120

Matthew 19:18–20   120-1

Matthew 19:21   121

Matthew 22:37–38   122

Matthew 22:39   123

Matthew 25:32–34   75

Matthew 25:46   76

Mark

Mark 4: 23–24   53

Mark 10:6–8   143

Mark 10:9   144

Mark 11:22   113

Mark 14:22-24   82

Mark 16:15–16   113

Luke

Luke 6:40   63

Luke 9:23   27

Luke 11:28   114

John

John 1:12   44

John 3:3   44

John 3:5   45 and 139

John 3:16   49 and 112

John 3:35   50

John 3:36   67

John 4:14   81

John 5:19   50

John 5:28–29   68

John 6:35   80-1

John 6:60-61   97

John 6:63   97

John 6:66   98

John 8:28   50

John 8:29   50

John 8:31–32   114

John 10:14–15, 27   75

John 10:30   57

John 10:34–36   58

John 10:37–38   59

John 12:25–26   112

John 13:34–35   124

John 14:2   116

John 14:6   31 and 131

John 14:15   115

John 14:21–23   125-6

John 14:26   9

John 14:27   127

John 15:4   119

John 15:4–5   32

John 15:10   115

John 16:13   55 and 135

John 16:25–27   70
John 17:3   69
John 17:20–23   60
John 20:27   109
John 20:29   109

Acts
Acts 2:38   113
Acts 4:12   136
Acts 5:32   114
Acts 10:43   113
Acts 17:28–29   42
Acts 24:15   68

Romans
Romans 3:23   36
Romans 8:16   43
Romans 8:17   43

1 Corinthians
1 Corinthians 11:11   144
1 Corinthians 15:29   147

2 Corinthians
2 Corinthians 6:17–18 51

Galatians
Galatians 4:7   45

Ephesians
Ephesians 2:8–9   119
Ephesians 2:20   138

Ephesians 3:5   138
Ephesians 4:11–13   137

Philippians
Philippians 2:5–6   59
Philippians 3:12   114

2 Thessalonians
2 Thessalonians 2:4   62

2 Timothy
2 Timothy 3:7   93
2 Timothy 3:16–17   6

Titus
Titus 1:2   70
Titus 2:14   38
Titus 3:7   67

Hebrews
Hebrews 2:10–11   64
Hebrews 5:4   140
Hebrews 5:8–9   122
Hebrews 6:1   159
Hebrews 7:11   142
Hebrews 7:25   37
Hebrews 9:15   116
Hebrews 10:1   39
Hebrews 10:10,14–15   39
Hebrews 11:1   91
Hebrews 12:9   41
Hebrews 13:8   155

James

James 1:12   129

1 Peter

1 Peter 3:7   144
1 Peter 4:6   146
1 Peter 4:10   152
1 Peter 5:6–7   129

2 Peter

2 Peter 1:3   54

1 John

1 John 2:25   116

Revelation

Revelation 2:7   79
Revelation 3:21–22   46
Revelation 12:7–9   13
Revelation 15:3   23
Revelation 21:7   51
Revelation 22:1–5   78-9
Revelation 22:12–14   80

About the Author

Kevin feels very blessed. He is grateful for the experiences of life.

He and his wife Valerie have six children. Raising them was fun, challenging, educational, and very rewarding. The six became twelve as each married. The twelve are now raising their children. Joy and love continue to expand. Kevin looks forward to continued life with Valerie as they age. He also looks forward to being with her for eternity.

Kevin loves nature. He enjoys learning about nature, and he enjoys being in it. He chose forestry as his profession. He worked many years "out in the woods". He transitioned to office work as a GIS programmer/analyst. He has a Bachelor of Science degree in Forestry and a Master of Science in Remote Sensing, specializing in GIS, both degrees from Utah State University.

As a boy, Kevin felt the Holy Spirit and committed to himself to live his life according to God's way. That decision shapes his life. He has sought and continues to seek to understand God's way and correct what is out of line within himself. He desires to be good.